NEW DIRECTIONS FOR MENTAL HEALTH SERVICES

H. Richard Lamb, *University of Southern California*
EDITOR-IN-CHIEF

Spirituality and Religion in Recovery from Mental Illness

Roger D. Fallot
Community Connections

EDITOR

Number 80, Winter 1998

JOSSEY-BASS PUBLISHERS
San Francisco

SPIRITUALITY AND RELIGION IN RECOVERY FROM MENTAL ILLNESS
Roger D. Fallot (ed.)
New Directions for Mental Health Services, no. 80
H. Richard Lamb, Editor-in-Chief

Microfilm copies of issues and articles are available in 16mm and 35mm, as well as microfiche in 105mm, through University Microfilms Inc., 300 North Zeeb Road, Ann Arbor, Michigan 48106-1346.

ISSN 0193-9416   ISBN 0-7879-4708-3

NEW DIRECTIONS FOR MENTAL HEALTH SERVICES is part of The Jossey-Bass Psychology Series and is published quarterly by Jossey-Bass Inc., Publishers, 350 Sansome Street, San Francisco, California 94104–1342.

SUBSCRIPTIONS cost $63.00 for individuals and $105.00 for institutions, agencies, and libraries.

EDITORIAL CORRESPONDENCE should be sent to the Editor-in-Chief, H. Richard Lamb, University of Southern California, Department of Psychiatry, Graduate Hall, 1937 Hospital Place, Los Angeles, California 90033-1071.

Cover photograph by Wernher Krutein/PHOTOVAULT © 1990.

Jossey-Bass Web address: www.josseybass.com

Printed in the United States of America on acid-free recycled paper containing 100 percent recovered waste paper, of which at least 20 percent is postconsumer waste.

CONTENTS

EDITOR'S NOTES

In the past twenty years, the value of constructive relations between the behavioral and medical sciences on the one hand and spirituality and religion on the other has become evident in the literature of both disciplines. In spite of this growing interest in the intersection of spirituality and mental health, however, the role of spirituality in the lives of people with severe mental disorders and in the services provided for them has been relatively neglected. This volume addresses the importance of increased attention to religious and spiritual dimensions of experience in developing and implementing mental health services that are responsive to the needs of individuals with serious mental illness. As comprehensive, empowerment-focused, and culturally attuned approaches to recovery and psychiatric rehabilitation become more widely adopted, the integration of spirituality can play a key role in mental health programs.

The role of religion and spirituality in mental health services should be expanded for many reasons. First, these dimensions are central to the self-understanding and recovery experiences of many consumers; understanding religion's place in a particular culture is often essential to offering culturally competent services; and research indicates that religion is often related to more positive mental health outcomes.

In outlining the place of spirituality and religion in recovery and in rehabilitation programs, Chapter One examines some of these reasons more fully and explores concerns raised by mental health professionals about incorporating spirituality in work with people who have serious mental illnesses. Chapter Two examines three key questions in the assessment of spirituality and religion in the context of severe mental disorders and sets the stage for the chapters that follow on mental health consumers' descriptions of their spiritual experiences. Because much of the interest in this domain has emerged from consumer perspectives, Chapters Three and Four offer two approaches to synthesizing the importance of spirituality as expressed in self-reports. Consumers' accounts of the various functions of spirituality provide important guides to offering assessment, planning, therapeutic, and rehabilitative services that are more sensitive to religious concerns.

Even when mental health agencies or providers are interested in expanding the place of spirituality in their services, it is not altogether obvious how to do so. Chapters Five, Six, and Seven offer ideas for particular services and collaborations. Chapter Five describes a long-standing group that is focused directly on the discussion of religious concerns and demonstrates one way a mental health program can effectively integrate spiritual issues in its services. The authors of Chapter Six, in contrast, describe a group that was *not* designed to address spirituality. Yet their "spiritually sensitive" approach recognizes spiritual dimensions in content and group process and illustrates a broad definition of spirituality in holistic mental health services. Chapter Seven describes the increasing possibilities for collaboration among faith communities, mental health organizations and agencies, and people with mental illness and specifies helpful guidelines for developing these relationships more fully.

Just as the clinical roles of spirituality and religion have often been neglected, the research literature has not taken adequate account of spirituality as a potentially powerful factor in both illness and well-being. Chapter Eight reviews the research on the relationship between religion and mental illness, demonstrates many of the positive connections between spirituality and health, and argues for more systematic inclusion of religious variables in studies of well-being among people with mental illness. Chapter Nine concludes with some brief suggestions for future work in this expanding field.

Roger D. Fallot
Editor

ROGER D. FALLOT is co-director of Community Connections and a member of the adjunct faculty in pastoral counseling at Loyola College in Maryland.

Mental health professionals have raised concerns about the role of spirituality and religion in services for people with severe mental disorders, but this chapter offers compelling reasons for increased attention to spiritual issues in service delivery.

The Place of Spirituality and Religion in Mental Health Services

Roger D. Fallot

There is a long history of mutual skepticism, if not antagonism, in the relationship between science and religion. As mental health practice became increasingly allied with natural science and rationalistic paradigms in the early twentieth century, many psychiatrists and psychologists wrote dismissively of spiritual or religious experience. Freud's (1927) characterization of religion as illusion and his analogy between religious ritual and obsessive-compulsive behaviors (1913) have come to represent a central fear of many spiritually committed people: that mental health professionals at best reduce religious conviction and practice to psychological processes and at worst actively derogate spirituality in its entirety.

Conversely, some religious people have adamantly denied the value of secular mental health services. Sharing the assumption of an inherent and irreducible conflict between scientific and religious worldviews, these individuals have counseled people to rely solely on religious sources of help for mental disorders and problems in living. Like the psychologists who reject a significant place for religion, these religionists reject a significant role for the human sciences.

In addition to the more extreme positions of mutual rejection, however, have been numerous attempts to find collaborative and integrative models for psychology and religion—models for theory, practice, and professional organization (see Vande Kemp, 1996, and Wulff, 1996, for helpful overviews of these diverse movements). Especially in the past twenty years, the value of constructive relations, both mutually supportive and mutually critical, between the behavioral and medical sciences on the one hand and between religion and spirituality on the other has become evident in the literature of both disciplines (for example, Browning, 1987; Shafranske, 1996a). Psychiatry's increased openness to recognizing the import of religion in clients' lives is evidenced in the DSM-IV inclusion of religious or spiritual problems as potentially appropriate foci of clinical attention (DSM-IV, 1994; Lukoff, Lu, and Turner, 1992). A committee recently developed and presented to the American Psychiatric Association a model curriculum for training psychiatric residents in religious issues (see Chapter Eight). Several book-length reviews have summarized and evaluated the literature relating religion to mental health or to clinical practice (Schumaker, 1992; Shafranske, 1996a; Pargament, 1997a; Koenig, 1998).

Despite this increased interest, however, little has been written about the place of religion and spirituality in the lives of people with severe mental illnesses. The first purpose of this chapter is to explore some of the concerns that have led to this relative neglect of spirituality in relation to serious mental illness, defined as schizophrenia, major depression, and bipolar and schizoaffective disorders. The second goal is to outline, by way of contrast, some of the clinical, theoretical, and empirical reasons for giving increased attention to spirituality in services for this population.

Definitional Issues

Definitions of *spirituality* and *religion* in both the clinical and research literatures have often been confusing and ambiguous. Attempts to refine these concepts for research purposes are ongoing (Zinnbauer and others, 1997). For some authors, religion is the more encompassing of the two constructs. Pargament (1997a), for example, sees religion as "the search for significance in ways related to the sacred" (p. 32), whereas spirituality refers to religion's most central function—the "search for the sacred" (p. 39).

For other writers, spirituality is the larger of the two concepts (Koenig, 1994) and may or may not include religion. The general approach among this group is to identify religion more or less closely with its institutional base. Religiousness, for instance, can refer to "adherence to the beliefs and practices of an organized church or religious institution" (Shafranske and Malony, 1990, p. 72). Spirituality, in this view, has primarily personal and experiential connotations. It may refer to a broad-based search for meaning and belonging in connection with core values (Sperry and Giblin, 1996) or to a relationship with a transcendent realm or being. From this perspective, personal spirituality may find expression in organized religious contexts, or it may remain outside these communities.

Because the ambiguities and multivalent meanings in these concepts are not likely to be resolved in the near future, it is important to be clear about each author's understanding and use of the terms. I will adopt a convention that emphasizes *experiential* and *institutional* dimensions. Experientially, both spirituality and religion may involve the following: a sense of ultimate meaning, purpose, and values; a relationship with a transcendent being or higher power; or a sense of the sacred or holy. In this way, one core traditional meaning of *religion* is virtually synonymous with *spirituality*. By that definition, a religious experience would not differ much conceptually from a spiritual experience.

An additional meaning of religion, though, is also necessary and refers to its institutional context. Here, religion may entail a defined set of beliefs (a doctrine), rituals, and practice, as well as an identifiable community of believers. Spirituality may also find group expression, but to the extent that group spiritual experience becomes formalized, it moves toward meeting the criteria for institutional religion.

Pargament (1997b) makes a compelling case for avoiding the dichotomy of good personal spirituality and bad institutional religion—an implicit bias in some models. The convention adopted in this chapter assumes no differential valuation of spirituality and religion. It further assumes that spirituality and religion both have personal, experiential dimensions and may have, to varying degrees of formal organization, communal expressions. When I wish to emphasize more formal religion as opposed to spiritual or religious experience, I will refer to it as organized or institutional religion.

Contextual Issues

Sociologists and historians of religion have pointed out the high level of religious involvement that characterizes the people of the United States. According to Finke and Stark (1992), there has been a gradual increase in participation in organized religion from the colonial period into the twentieth century, with current levels of religious adherence reaching nearly two-thirds of the population. Although specific religious groups and denominations have shifted markedly in size, the overall trend has been one of consistent growth. Immigration has added to the already tremendous range of Judeo-Christian expressions by bringing, among others, large and diverse numbers of Hindus, Muslims, Sikhs, and Buddhists.

Not only is there broad involvement in institutional religion in this country but there is a correspondingly prevalent set of beliefs about religion and its importance in daily life. Over 90 percent of the U.S. population say they believe in God, and nearly 90 percent report that they pray—the majority doing so daily (Gallup and Castelli, 1989; Hastings and Hastings, 1996). Measures of religious commitment might yield even stronger findings if a less institutional and traditional set of criteria were adopted—for example, if people who identified themselves as spiritual but not religious were included as well (Zinnbauer and others, 1997). In this broader social and cultural context, the relative inattention to matters of religion and spirituality in mental health programming is striking indeed. And given the movement of the past two decades toward more inclusive, multidimensional (holistic) assessments and the similarly comprehensive and integrated service arrangements in community-based treatment, the lack of attention to spirituality in the lives of mental health service consumers is all the more noteworthy.

Concerns About Religion and Spirituality in Mental Health Services

A wide variety of beliefs has limited the ways in which religion and spirituality might be addressed in services for people with severe mental disorders. A review of some of these factors is important to understanding the theoretical, clinical, and personal convictions that result in minimizing or avoiding religious issues.

First, as noted earlier, is the historical antagonism between the biobehavioral sciences and religion. In certain psychodynamic and cognitive-rational traditions, for example, religion is closely tied to maladaptive defensive functions, to irrational and distorted views of reality, or to automatically rigid and dogmatic patterns of thinking. On such theoretical grounds, some mental health professionals interpret religious experience as inherently regressive, primitive, or dysfunctional. Such concerns are often heightened in working with people who have severe mental illnesses and for whom delusions and hallucinations are not uncommon. In these cases, the clinician may have difficulty—both conceptually and clinically—in distinguishing, for example, between religious delusions and valid commitments (see Chapter Two).

Premature judgments rooted in a theoretical connection between religion and psychopathology fail to do justice to the multiple and diverse functions that religious and spiritual experience may play in the lives of consumers (see, for example, Sullivan, 1993). Literature that is both clinical and theoretical (for example, Meissner, 1984), as well as the research literature (Gartner, 1996; Schumaker, 1992), has demonstrated the complexity of the relationship between religion and psychosocial functioning. Before arriving at a conclusion about a consumer's religious or spiritual experience, clinicians need to make a careful assessment of the role of that experience in the consumer's overall life structure and functioning.

These difficulties in sorting through thorny questions of reality and illusion are related to a second concern raised by clinicians. For many professionals, addressing religion or spirituality is potentially disorganizing for people who may have (or have had at one time) delusional thoughts with religious content. And it may be confusing and counterproductive for many others because religious language is so often abstract, metaphorical, and symbolic. If one of the central cognitive deficits in the schizophrenic spectrum disorders is a failure to maintain adequate distance or to make necessary distinctions between the immediate and the abstract, this argument goes, then such discussions may undermine a more helpful focus on the concrete necessities of daily life.

Although it is certainly plausible that using language too closely allied with delusional thinking may lead to a strengthening of such content, there is little reason to single out religious language in this regard. Clearly, the clinical adoption of *any* language needs to be weighed in terms of its impact on, and relationship to, the consumer's beliefs and perceptions. In addition, it is probable that such concern with entrenching delusional processes is overdrawn. People with severe mental illnesses are rarely talked into, or out of, delusional beliefs. In fact, the sensitive exploration of these convictions may yield a great deal of important information for assessment and service planning (Fitchett, Burton, and Sivan, 1997). Again, appropriate concern with the process of such discussions is not addressed adequately by avoiding them altogether.

Similarly, the idea that using religious abstractions distracts people with severe mental disorders from daily realities rests on two questionable assumptions: (1) that it is possible to avoid such abstract language and (2) that religious abstractions automatically compete with concrete realities. Much language—religious and nonreligious—is metaphorical in nature; it is simply impossible to avoid analogies, metaphors, and abstractions in usual conversation. For clinicians, the key is to understand the impact a particular set of metaphors, symbols, or abstractions is likely to have on work with a particular consumer. Second, clinical interviews, psychotherapy experiences, and ongoing group discussions (see Chapter Five) indicate that most individuals with mental illness (when not acutely, severely psychotic) are not disorganized by exploring religious experience nor are they less able to attend to concrete daily tasks as a result of such exploration. For some individuals, in fact, having religious language available to them serves as a reinforcement for concentration on specific day-to-day challenges in areas such as substance abuse and trauma recovery (Fallot, 1997). Again, the clinical challenge is to understand the function of religious or spiritual language in the consumer's life rather than to reject such language on overgeneralized grounds.

A third factor in the relative neglect of religious and spiritual dimensions of consumers' lives may be the so-called religiosity gap between mental health professionals and the general public (Lukoff, Lu, and Turner, 1992). Organized religion and certain traditional religious beliefs apparently play a smaller role in the lives of psychologists and psychiatrists than in other people's lives. These mental health professionals tend to be notably less involved in institutional religion, less likely to believe in the existence of God, and less likely to see religion as important than the population as a whole (Lukoff, Lu, and Turner, 1992; Ragan, Malony, and Beit-Hallahmi, 1980; Shafranske, 1996b). Such findings are consistent with other large-scale surveys showing that with more education and higher occupational prestige, a "privatization" of religion and diminished involvement with conventional religiosity is more likely (Greer and Roof, 1992).

Although psychologists as a group thus differ from the general public in religious affiliation, participation, and particular beliefs, they are not especially negative about religion's overall role in human life. The majority of respondents in one survey of psychologists found that 53 percent saw religion as valuable, whereas only 14 percent considered it undesirable (Shafranske and Malony, 1990, p. 73). The relative lack of personal commitment to religion does not seem to generalize, then, to psychologists' views of religion as a dimension of people's experience. This may be partly due to the value psychologists place on *spirituality;* they consider it more personally relevant and generally salient than religion (Shafranske, 1996b). There does not appear to be a spirituality gap that is comparable to the gap in religious affiliation and belief (Lukoff, Lu, and Turner, 1992). In fact, one recent study found that, next to participants in New Age groups, mental health workers were most likely (44 percent) to identify themselves as "spiritual but not religious" (Zinnbauer and others, 1997). This differential commitment to spirituality may have two distinct implications. On the positive side, it may serve to enhance clinicians' acceptance of the varieties of religious and spiritual experience. On the negative side, to the extent that clinicians see themselves as valuing spirituality over religion, they may explicitly or implicitly communicate a negative bias toward organized religion in their clinical work.

In exploring the roles religion and spirituality may play in the lives of consumers and in mental health services, clinicians often raise other concerns: that discussing religion with consumers feels intrusive, that it seems too personal, or that it metaphorically appears to violate the separation of church and state. The larger contemporary culture provides considerable support for such concerns. Religion is often pictured as a deeply personal matter—a thoroughly private domain of conscience (or realm between self and God)—about which open discussion is discouraged. In the context of professional relationships, however, an arena in which an individual's history of sexual or physical abuse, current intimate relationships and sexual activities, daily financial details, grooming, and illegal drug use are frequent topics of conversation, it is ironic indeed that spiritual experiences may be thought of as too personal.

Exploring clinicians' concerns in this regard has shown that the anxiety about religious talk often rests on personal rather than cultural grounds. For some professionals, their own painful histories with organized religion or its representatives make any religious discussion difficult. Some express a sense of inadequacy, a lack of training in the face of unfamiliar language, or a lack of knowledge sufficient to address spiritual concerns. Most psychologists in one survey, for example, indicated agreement with the statement, "Psychologists, in general, do not possess the knowledge or skills to assist individuals in their religious or spiritual development" (Shafranske and Malony, 1990, p. 75). Faced with occasional pressure to validate or invalidate religious experiences ("You do believe that was a miracle, don't you?"), many clinicians choose to avoid this kind of topic entirely.

This final concern, though, is an argument for additional professional education and supervision in addressing religion and spirituality, not for avoiding the topics altogether. Bolstering clinicians' understanding of, and skill in responding to, religious material is the most effective antidote to its neglect.

Reasons to Include Religion and Spirituality in Mental Health Services

Given the range of concerns just described, it is not surprising that little attention has been paid to the role of spirituality in services for people with severe mental illness. However, there are several persuasive reasons for considering that role.

Reflects Consumer Self-Understanding. Religion and spirituality are central to the self-understanding of many consumers. Even though data are relatively sparse on the fuller meanings of religious commitment among people with severe mental disorders, the data available indicate that this population does not differ markedly from the larger public. Kroll and Sheehan (1989) found broad consistency between the religious beliefs and practices of a group of psychiatric inpatients and the general public. In a Community Connections survey of one hundred consumers, 94 percent indicated a belief in God or a higher power. Only 7 percent considered themselves "not at all religious," whereas over 70 percent said they were "moderately," "considerably," or "very" religious. Further, over 80 percent agreed or strongly agreed with the statement, "It is important for me to spend time in prayer," and 70 percent reported praying at least weekly (Fallot and Azrin, 1995). Because of the relatively greater involvement of African Americans in many aspects of religious activity (Gallup and Castelli, 1989), the large African American proportion of this sample may seem to inflate these figures. Other populations, however, indicate a similar commitment to religion or to spirituality. A survey by Eimer (1998) found parallel trends in a very different ethnic and regional group. Among predominantly white (65 percent) inpatients in a Michigan state psychiatric hospital, only 2 percent reported no belief in God, and 62 percent said they prayed at least weekly. Ritsher, Coursey, and Farrell (1997) note that many consumers spontaneously included religion among the most important "formative experiences" in their lives (following in frequency were relationships, work and accomplishments, and mental illness).

As is true for many other individuals, then, people with severe mental disorders may find in religion and spirituality deep sources of identity and meaning. Spirituality refers to who they *are* in addition to what they do and believe. For clinicians to minimize or avoid this dimension of experience, then, risks the neglect of a key aspect of self-definition for many consumers.

Facilitates Recovery. A second and closely related reason for including spirituality is that it may be central to the recovery experience of many consumers. Not only does religious commitment serve to clarify identity, it may function as a resource for personal and social strength (Fallot, 1997). As the paradigm of recovery (Anthony, 1993) has become more central in conceptualizing services for those with mental illness, emphases on enhanced self-esteem, greater empowerment, and a clearer sense of purpose have grown. Simultaneously, the necessity of looking at the full range of resources for recovery has also grown; spirituality is certainly prominent among these for many individuals. In Lindgren and Coursey's (1995) study, 80 percent of the consumer participants said that religion or spirituality had helped them in general, and 74 percent said that it helped when they were ill. Sullivan's interviews (1993; see Chapter Three) explore some of the reasons consumers give for their commitment to religion or spirituality, including strength for coping, social support, a sense of coherence, and the feeling of being a "whole person." Because recovery motifs are multidimensional and involve the entirety of an individual's life, it is not surprising that the encompassing realms of religion and spirituality may motivate, sustain, and consolidate the recovery process.

Enhances Cultural Sensitivity of Services. A third reason to include religion and spirituality in mental health services is the field's increasing awareness of the importance of culturally competent programming. In many cultural or subcultural and ethnic groups, religion and spirituality are especially vital sources of meaning and structure as well as healing. Many studies have pointed out, for example, the central role of black churches in the African American community (Lincoln and Mamiya, 1990). Pargament (1997a) has examined the greater use of religious coping mechanisms among those who are more religiously committed, including African Americans. He notes that religious coping, in turn, is most helpful for certain groups (blacks, the elderly, the poor, among others) who may have less access to other resources.

The clinician working with people from a cultural or ethnic group with strong religious beliefs and practices, then, needs to become knowledgeable about the function and meaning of these commitments. Mental health professions increasingly recognize this awareness as not only a clinical advantage but an ethical requirement. Most professional associations have established ethical codes that call for respect for the consumer's culture, and some specifically mention religion. Similarly, accreditation organizations increasingly recognize spiritual needs as part of an inclusive approach to services delivery.

Relates Positively to Psychosocial Well-Being The final rationale for increased attention to religion and spirituality is an empirical one. On the whole, there exists a trend toward a slight but positive relationship between most measures of religion and most measures of mental health (Masters and Bergin, 1992). Gartner (1996) summarizes work that has generally found religion to be related to "hard" measures of mental health: religiousness is connected to lower rates of suicide, drug and alcohol use, and depression. The research in this field, then, calls for greater attention to the potentially positive role that religion may play in psychosocial well-being.

Conclusion

There are many reasons to expand the role of religion and spirituality in mental health services; among them are the following: these dimensions are central to the self-understanding and recovery experiences of many consumers; understanding religion's place in a particular culture is often essential to offering culturally competent services; and research indicates that religion is often related to more positive mental health outcomes. As comprehensive, empowerment-focused, and culturally attuned approaches to recovery and psychiatric rehabilitation become more widely adopted, the integration of spirituality can play a key role in mental health programs for people with severe mental disorders.

References

Anthony, W. A. "Recovery from Mental Illness: The Guiding Vision of the Mental Health Service System in the 1990s." *Psychosocial Rehabilitation Journal,* 1993, *16* (4), 11–23.

Browning, D. S. *Religious Thought and the Modern Psychologies: A Critical Conversation in the Theology of Culture.* Philadelphia: Fortress Press, 1987.

Diagnostic and Statistical Manual of Mental Disorders, Fourth Edition. Washington, D.C.: American Psychiatric Association, 1994.

Eimer, K. W. "Religiosity among Patients with Severe Mental Illness at a State Psychiatric Hospital." Unpublished manuscript,Ypsilanti Regional Psychiatric Hospital, Ypsilanti, Michigan, 1998.

Fallot, R. D. "Spirituality in Trauma Recovery." In M. Harris (ed.), *Sexual Abuse in the Lives of Women Diagnosed with Serious Mental Illness.* Amsterdam: Harwood Academic Publishers, 1997.

Fallot, R. D., and Azrin, S. T. "Consumer Satisfaction: Findings from a Case Management Program Evaluation Study." Paper presented at the Annual Conference of the International Association of Psychosocial Rehabilitation Services, Boston, June 1995.

Finke, R., and Stark, R. *The Churching of America: 1776–1990.* New Brunswick, N.J.: Rutgers University Press, 1992.

Fitchett, G., Burton, L. A., and Sivan, A. B. "The Religious Needs and Resources of Psychiatric Inpatients." *The Journal of Nervous and Mental Disease,* 1997, *185* (5), 320–326.

Freud, S. *Totem and Taboo.* New York: Norton, 1950. (Originally published 1913.)

Freud, S. *The Future of an Illusion.* Garden City, N.Y.: Anchor Books, 1964. (Originally published 1927.)

Gallup, G., Jr., and Castelli, J. *The People's Religion: American Faith in the 90s.* New York: Macmillan, 1989.

Gartner, J. "Religious Commitment, Mental Health, and Prosocial Behavior: A Review of the Empirical Literature." In E. F. Shafranske (ed.), *Religion and the Clinical Practice of Psychology.* Washington, D.C.: American Psychological Association, 1996.

Greer, B. A., and Roof, W. C. "'Desperately Seeking Sheila': Locating Religious Privatism in American Society." *Journal for the Scientific Study of Religion,* 1992, *31* (3), 346–352.

Hastings, E. H., and Hastings, P. K. (eds.). *Index to International Public Opinion, 1994–95.* Westport, Conn.: Greenwood Press, 1996.

Koenig, H. G. *Aging and God: Spiritual Pathways to Mental Health in Midlife and Later Years.* New York: Haworth Press, 1994.

Koenig, H. G. *Handbook of Religion and Mental Health.* San Diego: Academic Press, 1998.

Kroll, J., and Sheehan, W. "Religious Beliefs and Practices Among 52 Psychiatric Inpatients in Minnesota." *American Journal of Psychiatry,* 1989, *146* (1), 67–72.

Lincoln, C. E., and Mamiya, L. H. *The Black Church in the African American Experience.* New York: Duke University Press, 1990.

Lindgren, K. N., and Coursey, R. D. "Spirituality and Serious Mental Illness: A Two-Part Study." *Psychosocial Rehabilitation Journal,* 1995, *18* (3), 93–111.

Lukoff, D., Lu, F., and Turner, R. "Toward a More Culturally Sensitive DSM-IV: Psychoreligious and Psychospiritual Problems." *The Journal of Nervous and Mental Disease,* 1992, *180* (11), 673–682.

Masters, K. S., and Bergin, A. E. "Religious Orientation and Mental Health." In J. F. Schumaker (ed.), *Religion and Mental Health.* New York: Oxford University Press, 1992.

Meissner, W. W. *Psychoanalysis and Religious Experience.* New Haven: Yale University Press, 1984.

Pargament, K. I. *The Psychology of Religion and Coping: Theory, Research, and Practice.* New York: Guilford Press, 1997a.

Pargament, K. I. "The Psychology of Religion *and* Spirituality? Yes and No." In M. J. Krejci (ed.), *Psychology of Religion Newsletter,* 1997b, *22* (3), 1–9.

Ragan, C., Malony, H. N., and Beit-Hallahmi, B. "Psychologists and Religion: Professional Factors and Personal Belief." *Review of Religious Research,* 1980, *21* (2), 208–217.

Ritsher, J.E.B., Coursey, R. D., and Farrell, E. W. "A Survey on Issues in the Lives of Women with Severe Mental Illness." *Psychiatric Services,* 1997, *48* (10), 1,273–1,282.

Schumaker, J.F. (ed.). *Religion and Mental Health.* New York: Oxford University Press, 1992.

Shafranske, E. F. (ed.). *Religion and the Clinical Practice of Psychology.* Washington, D.C.: American Psychological Association, 1996a.

Shafranske, E. F. "Religious Beliefs, Affiliations, and Practices of Clinical Psychologists." In Shafranske, E. F. (ed.), *Religion and the Clinical Practice of Psychology.* Washington, D.C.: American Psychological Association, 1996b.

Shafranske, E. F., and Malony, H. N. "Clinical Psychologists' Religious and Spiritual Orientations and their Practice of Psychotherapy." *Psychotherapy,* 1990, *27* (1), 72–78.

Sperry, L., and Giblin, P. "Marital and Family Therapy with Religious Persons." In E. F. Shafranske (ed.), *Religion and the Clinical Practice of Psychology.* Washington, D.C.: American Psychological Association, 1996.

Sullivan, W. P. "'It Helps Me to Be a Whole Person': The Role of Spirituality Among the Mentally Challenged." *Psychosocial Rehabilitation Journal,* 1993, *16* (3), 125–134.

Vande Kemp, H. "Historical Perspective: Religion and Clinical Psychology in America." In E. F. Shafranske (ed.), *Religion and the Clinical Practice of Psychology.* Washington, D.C.: American Psychological Association, 1996.

Wulff, D. W. "The Psychology of Religion: An Overview." In E. F. Shafranske (ed.), *Religion and the Clinical Practice of Psychology.* Washington, D.C.: American Psychological Association, 1996.

Zinnbauer, B. J., Pargament, K. I., Cole, B., Rye, M. S., Butter, E. M., Belavich, T. G., Hipp, K. M., Scott, A. B., and Kadar, J. L. "Religion and Spirituality: Unfuzzying the Fuzzy." *Journal for the Scientific Study of Religion,* 1997, *36* (4), 549–564.

ROGER D. FALLOT *is co-director of Community Connections in Washington, D.C., and a member of the adjunct faculty in pastoral counseling at Loyola College in Maryland.*

Assessing the role that religious or spiritual concerns play in the lives of people with severe mental disorders is crucial if clinicians are to determine whether those concerns can be successfully incorporated into service planning.

Assessment of Spirituality and Implications for Service Planning

Roger D. Fallot

One reason that spiritual and religious issues are avoided in mental health settings serving people with severe mental disorders is staff unfamiliarity or discomfort with the content of religious talk. How does a clinician understand religious experiences and language, especially if the clinician is from a different religious background, or has had painful experiences with religion, or has little interest in or commitment to spiritual concerns? The goal of this chapter is to provide ways to organize clinical thinking about religious and spiritual content in the context of severe mental illness and then to discuss briefly how spiritual issues may be incorporated into collaborative service planning with mental health consumers.

Categorizing Spiritual Experiences

Many mental health professionals want to know how to connect religious and spiritual concerns with commonly used diagnostic categories. DSM-IV (1994) offers three possibilities. First are instances in which religious experience or behavior is considered problematic *and* is attributable to a mental disorder. In these instances, the mental disorder is considered primary and the religious concern secondary or even epiphenomenal. The mental disorder is then coded on Axis I, and the religious problem is not identified separately in the formal diagnosis. Religious delusions and hallucinations are the clearest examples of this possibility. Examples are people who believe they are famous religious figures or who hear a devil's voice commanding them to carry out destructive acts. The most common understanding of this pattern is that the psychotic process is more basic and that the delusional content—religious or otherwise—is drawn from the person's cultural context, either as an extension of, or active rejection of, religiocultural beliefs (Lowe, 1954; Argyle and Beit-Hallahmi, 1975).

The second alternative is that the religious content is problematic and worthy of clinical attention but *not* attributable to a mental disorder. DSM-IV includes a V Code (V62.89) for use with a religious or spiritual problem such as the distress related to "the loss or questioning of faith, problems associated with conversion to a new faith, or questioning of spiritual values . . ." (p. 685). After determining that the spiritual problem is not attributable to a mental disorder, the clinician's task is to decide whether or not the particular concern warrants attention in the mental health setting.

Lukoff, Lu, and Turner (1992), in a pre-DSM-IV article, label "psychoreligious" and "psychospiritual" problems those concerns with religion or spirituality that may be helpfully addressed by mental health professionals. They distinguish these from the "purely religious or spiritual problems" (p. 677) for which help is usually sought from and offered by clergy or spiritual specialists. For the assessing clinician, the task in these instances is to decide whether the psychosocial correlates of a religious concern are such that a mental health response is appropriate—in addition to, or in place of, that of a religious professional.

It is important to recognize that for many people with severe mental disorders, religious issues may be cause for distress but are not themselves expressions of a mental illness. These include the entire range of concerns that people without mental illness may have about religion (for example, how to deal with personal or family conflict about religion or how to cope with changes in spiritual convictions or practice). They also include concerns that are secondary to mental health consumers' psychiatric problems and to social stigma (for example, being excluded or marginalized in faith communities, feeling shame about periods of religious disengagement, or having difficulties sorting through religious aspects of acute psychotic experience).

The use of DSM-IV carries important implications for the *contextual* nature of assessment in sorting out these first two possibilities. First, DSM-IV takes some important steps in dealing with the relationship between psychopathology and cultural or religious material. It recognizes, for example, that judgments about the diagnostic significance of religious experiences cannot be separated from the cultural context of the individual being assessed. It illustrates the consequences of a clinician's lack of cultural sensitivity and competence by pointing out the possible misdiagnosis of certain religious practices and beliefs as evidence of a psychotic disorder (p. xxiv). And it further acknowledges in Appendix I that unique cultural patterns may account for specific beliefs and practices more accurately than generalized judgments based on universalized psychiatric "symptoms," drawing on several examples of spirituality's functions as both explanatory framework and social structure.

It is difficult to overstate the significance of this attention to cultural processes in understanding religious expression. Lukoff, Lu, and Turner (1995) emphasize the importance of understanding the person's basic religious convictions and that of his or her religious community in order to assess psychopathology adequately. Any judgment about the meaning of spiritual or religious experiences and behavior must take into consideration the sociocultural context of both the assessor and the assessed. One woman with strong religious commitments, for example, was diagnosed with a psychotic disorder and was homeless for a period. During this time, she had a "religious experience" in which she felt warmed and protected by a visible light from God that sustained her through a very cold and lonely night. After she had been in treatment for some time and her recurrent psychiatric symptoms were well controlled, however, she still needed to discuss whether or not this experience was a valid miracle. In this discussion, it became apparent that her concern with this experience being designated as miraculous was more connected to her religiocultural background and current involvements than to a mental disorder. Taking such a need seriously in the evaluative and planning process enabled the person doing the assessment to avoid inappropriate pathologizing of either her experience or her concern with its labeling.

The second implication of DSM-IV use is that the assessment of spirituality must also take into account the person's overall functioning. In a culture where it is increasingly common to read public accounts of religious motives for a tremendous range of behaviors, it is often difficult to understand the nuances of spiritual meanings. Lukoff, Lu, and Turner (1995) summarize proposed criteria for distinguishing between "psychopathology and authentic spiritual experiences" (p. 471). They emphasize, for instance, a set of indicators related to good prognosis: good pre-episode functioning, acute onset and stressful precipitants, and a positive exploratory attitude toward the experience.

The tendency among some mental health professionals, though, is to assume that religious motives are psychopathologically suspect until proven otherwise. This perspective is sometimes fueled by assumptions of the pervasiveness of delusional or hallucinatory experiences among people with severe mental illnesses and by the ready connection between religious ideation and delusion. It is sometimes fueled by concern with liability related to command hallucinations (for example, an individual whose homicidal or suicidal impulses are attributed to the voice of either God or the devil). In one illustrative instance, a housing program interviewer asked a consumer whom the consumer would talk to if she needed assistance in dealing with problems in her prospective apartment. The woman, who was devoutly religious, responded that she would talk to God. The interviewer understood this as a reflection of the consumer's poor reality-testing ability, as well as her deficient judgment, and rejected the housing application.

But comprehensive assessment requires attention to overall psychological organization; to functioning in social, vocational, educational, familial, and other roles; to biological syndromes; and to the synthesis of these with religious or spiritual experiences. Only in this overall functional context can a judgment be made about the specific place of spirituality. In the housing decision just described, for instance, additional questions ("Is there anyone else you would talk to?" or "What do you think God would do?" or "What else would you do?" or "How would you deal with other problems?") might have clarified whether the housing applicant's problem-solving skills were adversely affected by her religious beliefs.

A primary source of difficulty in assessing the role of religious or spiritual experience, then, is decontextualization. Appropriate decisions about categorizing religious experience require careful attention to the larger cultural context and to a comprehensive biopsychosocial assessment of the individual's functioning.

There is of course an implicit third alternative for religious experience in relation to DSM-IV: not addressing spirituality because its expression is neither attributable to a mental disorder nor problematic enough to require clinical attention. DSM-IV is not designed to assess spirituality or religion in other than a problem-focused way. But for many people with severe mental illness, spirituality is more a resource than a difficulty. And it may have more significant implications for service planning as an area of goal development (for example, to engage or re-engage with a faith community) than it does as a focus of clinical treatment. This recognition is significant because of the bias that often assimilates religious talk among people with mental illness to their psychopathology. Although there may be some reason for this predisposition in the assessment of acute psychotic episodes (where virtually any content domain may be subject to distortion), there is no compelling evidence that religiousness per se is more problematic than any other domain of experience for people recovering from mental illness. In fact, clinical reports indicate that individuals who are not acutely psychotic can gain a great deal from the exploration of spirituality (see Chapter Five). A more comprehensive assessment of spirituality, then, moves beyond the mental disorder categorization in DSM-IV to consider more broadly the place of spirituality in the life of the consumer.

Evaluating Spiritual Experiences

A second key question for mental health professionals who are assessing spirituality is, To what degree is this expression of spirituality consistent with overall well-being? The assessment emphasis shifts from *categorizing* spiritual experience in relation to psychiatric syndromes to *evaluating* spirituality in relation to models of general psychosocial health and maturity.

Most frameworks for answering this question are based in the psychology of religion literature (see Schumaker [1992], Wulff [1991], or Pargament [1997] for more comprehensive treatments). These models all frame the understanding of religious experience in relationship to some criteria for mental health. One of the best known and well researched of these models is that of Allport (1950; Allport and Ross, 1967). For Allport, religious experience was most helpfully evaluated in motivational terms. Extrinsic commitments reflect the "use" of religion to meet primarily social or personal needs. Examples of this are to form interpersonal networks or to find comfort and be soothed. Intrinsic commitments, however, express motives for religion for its own sake, as in this intrinsic item from his scale: "My whole life is based on my religion." The differential valuation in Allport's system resides in an assumption of greater maturity and health that is related to intrinsic motives for any human behavior. Intrinsic religion is better than extrinsic religion because it is more mature in its motivational roots. The validity of this judgment is strengthened by the empirical relationship between intrinsic religion and indicators of mental health such as flexibility and lower authoritarianism.

Writers have brought many such psychological models to bear in evaluating spirituality: object relations theory (Meissner, 1984); family systems theory (Friedman, 1985); coping theory (Pargament, 1997), among many others. Such frameworks offer a vivid reminder of the importance of clarifying the *values* and the specific *criteria* involved in making judgments about the psychological worth of any spiritual experience. (Remember that all of these approaches involve the application of social science criteria to the evaluation of religion. This is very different from evaluating religious claims on their own terms, which is a theological or spiritual task.) Julian (1987) offers one example of using resources from the tradition of Christian spiritual discernment in distinguishing "authentic" from "pathological" religious experiences in psychiatric patients.

Many clinicians who want to understand the spiritual aspects of experience become discouraged at the lack of clarity about the apparently positive and negative roles that religion may play in the lives of people with severe mental illness. Explicit ways to evaluate the role of religious experience in individuals' lives thus become essential. Howard Clinebell (1984), drawing on a broad range of psychological, social, and theological sources, has developed one of the more inclusive sets of value criteria for assessing the extent to which spirituality is positive and growth enhancing. He specifies twenty-three questions covering a broad range of life domains and experiences. Some deal with the individual's sense of self (for example, do the person's spiritual beliefs, attitudes, and practices "foster self-esteem and the 'owning'. . . of [his or her] strengths?"; "Do they stimulate the growth of . . . inner freedom and autonomy?") p. 118. Others address a sense of life's meaning (Does the person's spirituality give him or her a "meaningful philosophy of life that provides trust and hope in facing the inevitable tragedies of life?" Does spirituality "foster realistic hope by encouraging the acceptance rather than the denial of reality?") p. 118. A third group is more relational in focus (Does the person's spiritual life help him or her "develop" relationships committed to mutual growth?" Does it offer the person a "growth-enabling community of caring?") p. 118. Other questions deal with transcendence more directly (Does spirituality "nurture the transcendent dimensions" of the person's life—of his or her "higher Self?") p. 118. Finally, some criteria are related to ethics (Does spirituality "provide creative values and ethical sensitivities that serve as inner guidelines for behavior that is both personally and socially responsible?") p. 118.

The point of describing this model in some detail is only partly to commend its content. Whatever evaluative schema are adopted, it is important to make often-implicit values explicit (Bergin, 1980; Ellis, 1980, 1992). That is, in deciding the degree to which spirituality plays a positive or negative role in an individual's life, the assessment process needs to be clear about the grounds on which such a judgment rests. Whether adopting the criteria, then, of a particular theory of personality and psychopathology (such as object relations) or of an empirically derived model (such as effective psychosocial coping) or of a multidimensional statement of core values (such as Bergin's [1980] or Clinebell's [1984]), useful spiritual assessment requires awareness of the framework for human functioning that underlies its evaluative process. As Bergin (1980) and Browning (1987), among others, have pointed out, it is impossible for the social sciences to claim value neutrality; it is important, however, to develop value clarity. Nowhere is this more evident than in addressing religious and spiritual concerns.

Interpreting the Functions of Spiritual Experiences

Some of the most important and least frequently asked questions about spirituality in the lives of people with severe mental illness shift the emphasis from *categorizing* and *evaluating* to *describing* and *interpreting* the various dimensions of spiritual experience, as well as the functions that spirituality may fill in an individual's life.

Writers have proposed many models for this type of spiritual assessment. Psychologists of religion have developed descriptive frameworks (for example, Pruyser, 1976; Malony, 1992). Others have been formulated in fields with which many mental health professionals are unfamiliar, such as nursing (for example, Carpenito, 1997) and pastoral care (for example, Fitchett, 1993; Eimer, 1989; Weiss, 1991).

Fitchett's (1993) approach represents one of the most thoughtful and comprehensive examples of this work. The spiritual dimension is one of seven life domains (holistic dimensions) included in the overall assessment; the others are the medical, psychological, psychosocial, family systems, ethnic, cultural, and societal issues. The spiritual domain is also described in seven dimensions. To describe these dimensions, the person completing the assessment may draw on individuals' self-reports, behavioral priorities, and implicit and explicit commitments. The first spiritual dimension is "beliefs and meaning"; the goal is to understand and summarize the ways in which an individual finds and creates a sense of purpose and meaning in life. The second dimension is "vocation and consequences," referring to the individual's sense of duty and obligation, as well as the results of fulfilling or failing to fulfill these obligations. Third is "experience and emotion," addressing the overall emotional tone of the person's spiritual life, as well as any direct spiritual experiences. "Courage and growth" is the fourth aspect of spirituality and refers to one's capacity to face doubt and to be open to change. The "rituals and practices" expressing the person's key beliefs or obligations is the fifth category. The individual's life in "community" reflects the person's participation in formal or informal communities that share belief or practice. Finally, the person's sources of "authority and guidance" for their core beliefs are the seventh dimension.

For the purposes of spiritual assessment with people who have severe mental disorders, there are several advantages to approaches such as Fitchett's. First, this model prioritizes a *functional* assessment method, focusing primarily on *how* a person finds meaning and secondarily on *what* a person believes in relation to some specific content (for example, a God-image or prayer). This enhances its generalizability across different belief systems and is especially useful in pluralistic settings. Second, it permits, even requires, the person doing the assessment to be an active interpreter of the individual's spiritual life. It does not rely only on unidimensional and forced-choice self-reports and therefore is more likely to fit with the larger process of service planning. Third, it assumes that there is a spiritual dimension in each individual's life by adopting an implicitly broad definition of spirituality; this permits its use with individuals who do not label themselves as spiritual or religious, as well as with those who do. Fourth, this model makes no assumptions about the inherent value of a particular spiritual orientation in terms of its function in the overall context of a person's life.

A Spiritual Assessment Model

Community Connections, in response to staff and consumer interest and to growing expectations from accrediting organizations for attention to spirituality, began to explore models for incorporating spiritual assessment more consistently in the service planning process. As an urban, not-for-profit mental health agency working with marginalized people who have severe mental illnesses, we set several criteria for a useful and feasible assessment method in this setting. First, we wanted a framework useful for work with people from many different religious traditions, as well as with people who do not describe themselves as religious or spiritual. We also wanted a tool that acknowledges that spirituality may play a negative as well as positive role for any individual at a particular time. We wanted a blend of quantitative and qualitative data for the purpose of following more systematically any changes in the spiritual dimension over time. It was important to adopt an assessment appropriate for clinician-providers who had no specialized training in spirituality or religion beyond the instrument itself. We sought a simple and brief method that could be easily incorporated into discussions with consumers and periodic comprehensive assessment points. Finally, we wanted to make explicit the connections between spiritual assessment and service planning.

With these criteria in mind, Community Connections staff developed and have begun to pilot a spiritual assessment method that is appropriate for our setting (Fallot, Freeman, and Hayden, 1997). Beginning with an adaptation of Fitchett's (1993) model, its goals are several: (1) to understand on four dimensions key aspects of the individual's spiritual life; (2) to assess the extent to which these aspects are framed in traditional religious language and activities; (3) to assess the extent to which spirituality contributes to, or undermines, the individual's overall well-being; (4) to assess the extent to which religious or spiritual content is connected to psychotic process; (5) to make more readily accessible the connections between spiritual assessment and collaborative service planning with consumers.

Exhibit 2.1 shows the first page of the assessment. The clinician completing the assessment may or may not write a narrative summary of the four dimensions to accompany the ratings; the primary goal of these categories is to help organize the clinician's consideration and understanding of the consumer's spiritual experience.

The second page focuses on contextual questions. It asks, for instance, about the extent to which the clinician and consumer have explicitly discussed issues of spirituality or religion, about how important the clinician thinks spirituality is in the consumer's life, about the extent to which religious or spiritual experiences are part of psychotic symptoms, and about the inclusion of spirituality in service planning. It asks whether the issues were discussed as a *problem area* (for example, spiritual struggles or religious activities that conflict with other important goals), a *goal* (for example, reconnection to a religious community or the development of religious practice more consistent with other plans), or a *resource* (for example, for coping with short- or long-term stress).

Preliminary reports from a number of clinicians and care coordinators indicate that this framework has been helpful in shaping a clearer approach to talking about and thinking through consumers' spiritual experiences. These clinicians say that their discussions of spirituality have become more focused. They have generally not felt that they were encroaching on the professional territory of clergy or spiritual specialists. Clinicians need to remain within the parameters of their professional expertise and training. Mental health professionals' role in spiritual assessment is not to become a religious specialist any more than their discussing consumers' physical problems and strengths implies becoming a physician. On the contrary, because the assessment is framed in descriptive and functional terms, the clinician's goal is consistent with holistic approaches: understanding the consumer's experience and then collaborating in deciding whether and how to incorporate spirituality in service planning. Sometimes there is no identified spiritual problem, goal, or resource for planning purposes. Sometimes an identified spiritual problem or goal can be addressed by the consumer alone; sometimes it involves referral to religious professionals; sometimes it is incorporated into psychosocial treatment. Having a clear and shared understanding about spirituality assists the clinician and consumer to discuss more fully its place in psychiatric rehabilitation and recovery.

Developing a method for spiritual assessment involves attention to local knowledge: the unique characteristics of the consumers and clinicians involved in the assessment process. A format such as Fitchett's or the Community

Exhibit 2.1. Community Connections Spiritual Assessment

Definitions: Spirituality or religion may refer to one's ultimate values; a sense of meaning and purpose; relationship with the sacred or divine or higher power; a sense of the holy or transcendent; and/or a unifying, integrating, or vitalizing dimension of experience. Organized religion refers to the expression of spiritual or religious experience in a set of symbols; defined beliefs or doctrines; an identifiable community of believers; and specific rituals and/or practices.

Spiritual/Religious Domain	Explicitness of Religious Language	Role in Client's Overall Well-Being
	"How often are the experiences in this domain expressed in the language or practices of a particular organized religious tradition?" 1 = not at all religious 2 = occasionally religious 3 = often religious 4 = usually religious 5 = always religious	"What role do the client's experiences in this domain play in his or her overall well-being?" 1 = consistently undermine well-being 2 = often undermine 3 = neither undermine nor enhance well-being or both undermine and enhance 4 = usually enhance well-being 5 = consistently enhance well-being
Beliefs and Meaning: Consider how the client makes sense of her or his life experience; how a sense of meaning or purpose is expressed in life; how behavior may reflect a sense of vitality, direction, and values; how key stories may capture core beliefs about life's meaning.		
Experience and Emotion: Consider the overall emotional tone of the client's spiritual life (does the person feel grateful or resentful, joyful or despairing, timid or courageous, guilty or accepted, worthless or valuable?); any direct encounter or ongoing relationship with the divine or higher power.		
Rituals and Practice: Consider the rituals or activities which give expression to the client's sense of meaning and purpose; the practices which are part of fulfilling important duties or obligations in his or her life; practices around which there is notable energy in the client's life.		
Community: Consider the client's membership and participation in any formal or informal communities of shared belief and meaning in life, or of shared ritual and practice; consider communities which may be based on religion, therapy/support, work, family, or friendship.		

Note: Adapted from Fitchett 1993

Connections' adaptation and elaboration may serve as a starting point for understanding the spiritual needs of consumers in programs for people with severe mental disorders. Tailoring questions and planning to the specific context, however, enhances the usefulness of any such assessment tool.

Conclusion

Assessment of spirituality and religion may serve a number of functions for the mental health professional. In addition to placing spirituality in relationship to accepted diagnostic groupings and judging its value in relationship to an individual's overall well-being, the clinician may seek, with the consumer, to understand spirituality's roles in the consumer's life and to consider whether and how spirituality should be included in a comprehensive plan for needed services.

References

Allport, G. W. *The Individual and His Religion.* New York: Macmillan, 1950.

Allport, G. W., and Ross, J. M. "Personal Religious Orientation and Prejudice." *Journal of Personality and Social Psychology,* 1967, 5 (4), 432–443.

Argyle, M., and Beit-Hallahmi, B. *The Social Psychology of Religion.* London: Routledge and Kegan Paul, 1975.

Bergin, A. E. "Psychotherapy and Religious Values." *Journal of Consulting and Clinical Psychology,* 1980, 48 (1), 95–105.

Browning, D. S. *Religious Thought and the Modern Psychologies: A Critical Conversation in the Theology of Culture.* Philadelphia: Fortress Press, 1987.

Carpenito, L. J. "Spiritual Distress." In *Nursing Diagnosis: Application to Clinical Practice.* Philadelphia: Lippincott, 1997, 852–870.

Clinebell, H. *Basic Types of Pastoral Care and Counseling.* Nashville: Abingdon Press, 1984.

Diagnostic and Statistical Manual of Mental Disorders, Fourth Edition. Washington, D.C.: American Psychiatric Association, 1994.

Eimer, K. W. "The Assessment and Treatment of the Religiously Concerned Psychiatric Patient." *The Journal of Pastoral Care,* 1989, XLIII (3), 231–241.

Ellis, A. "Psychotherapy and Atheistic Values: A Response to A. E. Bergin's 'Psychotherapy and Religious Values,'" *Journal of Consulting and Clinical Psychology,* 1980, 48 (5), 635–639.

Ellis, A. "My Current Views of Rational-Emotive Therapy (RET) and Religiousness." *Journal of Rational-Emotive and Cognitive-Behavior Therapy,* 1992, 10 (1), 37–40.

Fallot, R. D., Freeman, D., and Hayden, J. "A Spiritual Assessment Method for Community Connections." Unpublished manuscript, Community Connections, Washington, D.C., 1997.

Fitchett, G. *Assessing Spiritual Needs: A Guide for Caregivers.* Minneapolis: Augsburg Fortress, 1993.

Friedman, E. H. *Generation to Generation: Family Process in Church and Synagogue.* New York: Guilford Press, 1985.

Julian, R. "Spiritual Discernment in Psychiatric Patients." *Journal of Religion and Health,* 1987, 26 (2), 125–130.

Lowe, W. L. "Group Beliefs and Socio-Cultural Factors in Religious Delusions." *The Journal of Social Psychology,* 1954, 40, 267–274.

Lukoff, D., Lu, F., and Turner, R. "Toward a More Culturally Sensitive DSM-IV: Psycho-religious and Psychospiritual Problems." *The Journal of Nervous and Mental Disease,* 1992, *180* (11), 673–682.

Lukoff, D., Lu, F., and Turner, R. "Cultural Considerations in the Assessment and Treatment of Religious and Spiritual Problems." *Cultural Psychiatry,* 1995, *18* (3), 467–485.

Malony, H. N. "Religious Diagnosis in Evaluations of Mental Health." In J. F. Schumaker (ed.), *Religion and Mental Health.* New York: Oxford University Press, 1992.

Meissner, W. W. *Psychoanalysis and Religious Experience.* New Haven: Yale University Press, 1984.

Pargament, K. I. *The Psychology of Religion and Coping: Theory, Research, and Practice.* New York: Guilford Press, 1997.

Pruyser, P. *The Minister as Diagnostician.* Philadelphia: Westminster Press, 1976.

Schumaker, J. F. (ed.) *Religion and Mental Health.* New York: Oxford University Press, 1992.

Weiss, F. S. "Pastoral Care Planning: A Process-Oriented Approach for Mental Health Ministry." *The Journal of Pastoral Care,* 1991, *XLV* (3), 268–278.

Wulff, D. W. *Psychology of Religion: Classic and Contemporary Views.* New York: Wiley, 1991.

ROGER D. FALLOT is co-director of Community Connections in Washington, D.C., and a member of the adjunct faculty in pastoral counseling at Loyola College in Maryland.

Because many consumers view spirituality as important in their recovery, mental health professionals can benefit from a clearer understanding of the role of religion from the consumer's perspective.

Recoiling, Regrouping, and Recovering: First-Person Accounts of the Role of Spirituality in the Course of Serious Mental Illness

W. Patrick Sullivan

Serious and persistent mental illness remains a mystery to those attempting to unravel its causes and cures and is still largely misunderstood by the general public. Nonetheless, with each passing day more is learned about the origins of illnesses like schizophrenia, and advances in psychopharmacology and community treatment are giving affected individuals a real opportunity to be active players in daily community discourse.

However, what may be perceived as a vexing research question, a tax on community resources, or a subject of moral and ethical debates is still experienced at the personal level. Serious mental illness poses a threat to personhood and self like few other illnesses. By affecting every facet of life—from thought processes, to the ability to survive in the marketplace, to an increased susceptibility to exploitation and restrictions on individual choice and movement—serious mental illness presents a challenge that is difficult to overcome. Cooper (1993) offers a reminder of the hurdle that consumers face: "The biomedical model of mental illness has contributed significantly to our understanding of major mental illness, but little to true recovery. While medications may help one's behaviors become more acceptable to society, they do nothing to put one's shattered soul back together" (p. 15).

In our incessant and necessary attempts to understand the mechanics of serious mental illness, we often lose touch with those who matter most—the persons trying to make sense of their lives and to survive on a day-by-day basis. Not only is losing touch problematic from a humanistic viewpoint but an important source of information about the course of the illness and recovery process is ignored. Estroff (1992) argues that we should "learn about the various ways that people who have schizophrenia live in the world, actually and symbolically, in their own terms" (pp. 280–281). Armed with this knowledge, we may then have a better grasp on the experience of serious mental illness and use this knowledge to aid those in the process of recovery.

Kleinman (1988) vividly describes an experience, during his medical training, of working with a badly burned child. After trying to distract the young girl from the pain she was enduring on a daily basis to no effect, he decided to talk with her directly about her experience. Reflecting on this event he notes: "She taught me a grand lesson in patient care: that it is possible to talk with patients, even those who are most distressed, about the actual experience of illness, and that witnessing and helping to order that experience can be of therapeutic value" (p. xii).

Recovery from Serious and Persistent Mental Illness

In the past decade the concept of *chronicity*—a previously accepted feature of serious mental illnesses like schizophrenia—has been challenged. Longitudinal research demonstrates that many people diagnosed with serious mental illnesses improve, at times, without extensive professional intervention (Harding, Zubin, and Strauss, 1992). Cross-cultural studies also suggest that the course of serious mental illness might vary by locale (Sullivan, 1994a). The accumulation of research, the experience of practitioners, and the collective voice of many current and former consumers of mental health services have all contributed to a re-evaluation of previously held beliefs about mental illness. From this experience an important term—*recovery*—was added to the lexicon of those concerned about serious mental illnesses. Anthony (1993) notes that recovery "is a deeply personal, unique process of changing one's attitude, values, feelings, goals, skills, and/or roles. It is a way of living a satisfying, hopeful, and contributing life even with the limitations caused by illness" (p. 15).

The vision of recovery embodies a more optimistic prognosis for those who face neurobiological disorders and also posits an active role for the individual in shaping a life course. The recovery paradigm also affords an opportunity to explore problems and issues from a fresh perspective: new questions can now be posed and new methods employed to try to answer them.

Estroff (1994) stresses the importance of asking the right questions in our quest to understand the lived experience of mental illness. So often what we know—or think we know—about these disorders has been shaped by the nature of the questions we have asked, and even how we have asked them. If the experience of serious mental illness and the course of the recovery process is deeply personal, the best sources of knowledge are those individuals struggling to recover. And this knowledge, particularly in the formative stages, cannot be drawn simply from responses to a set of predetermined questions but instead must reflect the life story of informants.

The research that serves as the centerpiece of this chapter began before the term *recovery* had emerged in the literature (see Sullivan, 1994b, for a detailed description of the study and the results). It was inspired by both empirical research and direct practice, all of which suggested that many people previously considered to be chronically mentally ill did improve and live satisfying lives.

The study was an early attempt to learn from those who appeared to be surmounting the effects of serious mental illness. Success, for purposes of this study, was reflected by the actual behaviors of consumers—a potential limitation that will be addressed later. The respondents had remained free from psychiatric hospitalization for over two years, lived in at least a semi-independent setting, and were engaged in some form of vocational activity. Informants were referred by mental health professionals, family members, or self.

Fifty-four current and former consumers of mental health services participated in a semistructured interview that lasted approximately one hour. To be included in the study, respondents matched the criteria for severe and persistent mental illness captured in the basic dimensions of diagnosis, duration, and disability. Of the original sample, forty-six respondents met the criteria for inclusion in the study, based on their diagnosis and psychiatric history, as well as their current level of functioning. The respondents were nearly evenly split between males and females and were predominantly white; the most common diagnosis was schizophrenia (74 percent), and respondents had averaged a lifetime total of 5.6 psychiatric hospitalizations. Significantly, the average length of time since their previous psychiatric hospitalization was six years.

Informants were asked to share the factors that contributed to their success in dealing with a mental illness. All interviews were recorded and transcribed verbatim, and respondents were paid for sharing their expertise. The responses were subsequently analyzed using elements of Spradley's (1979) ethnographic interviewing method. The use of qualitative methodology was consciously chosen in order to elicit data entirely from the respondents' perspectives. This method allows for unforeseen data to emerge and recognizes the consumer as the expert on the recovery process.

Several of the factors identified by respondents as critical to their success were predictable: medication, vocational activity, professional helpers, and the support of family and friends. An unforeseen finding, however, was that 43 percent of respondents indicated that spirituality (broadly defined, thus encompassing organized religious practices) was important in their recovery process.

Such a finding likely engenders a range of emotions among professionals. Certainly, most practitioners who have worked with those suffering from serious mental illness have encountered highly delusional consumers who have become obsessively preoccupied with religious thoughts to the point that they believed they were God. And even though there have been points of interchange between mental health professionals and the clergy, the relationship, historically, can best be described as delicate (Giglio, 1993).

In spite of the problems with religiosity among consumers and unfortunate differences among professionals, it is clear that personal spirituality is vitally important and offers genuine help to many who face serious and persistent mental illnesses. Spirituality can serve as a primary coping and problem-solving device (Ellison, 1991; Michello, 1988; Pargament and others, 1990). It can also be an important aspect of a personal social support network (Maton, 1989; Pollner, 1989; Sullivan, 1992) and can help sustain a sense of coherence and meaning in life (Allport, 1963; Idler, 1987; Petersen and Roy, 1985; Titone, 1991). In the following sections the specific ways that spirituality is helpful will be explored, drawing from first-person accounts.

Spirituality in the Coping and Decision-Making Process

It is often noted that people who have serious mental illness are vulnerable to stress. Certainly, the experience of dealing with mental illness is stressful, particularly given the confusion and difficulty in organizing one's thoughts that accompanies illnesses like schizophrenia. For many, religion and spirituality provide a buffer from such stress (Hathaway and Pargament, 1990). At times, the ability to cope is augmented by specific activities such as prayer. One respondent noted that when times get tough, "I just go to bed and say about fifty prayers . . . it just relaxes me." Another consumer who suffers from panic attacks uses the same approach: "I can pray and ask the Lord to get rid of the voices and help me relax."

A related aspect of coping involves making decisions and taking actions that support recovery. This includes taking a proactive stance toward life and acknowledging that managing one's illness requires some alterations in behaviors and attitudes. It has been proposed that spirituality and religion have an indirect influence on health by steering individuals away from risky behaviors or from conduct that alienates them from others (Dull and Skokan, 1995; Idler, 1987). For example, several respondents suggested that their spiritual beliefs helped them avoid alcohol and drug use—a common factor in relapse and recidivism. One informant said that "the grace of God is what keeps me sober today."

Religious figures or precepts also provide role models or guides to follow. This seemed particularly important for informants who recognized that their behavior could be problematic for themselves and for others. To illustrate, one respondent noted that "Jesus is an example to all of us and he lived his life completely pure and honest, just a good man . . . and you know, why not pattern your life after him?" In a similar vein, another person noted that "religion has taught me to not go off and pout and stuff, just stay on an even keel."

Spirituality and Social Support

Loneliness and isolation are unfortunate realities in the lives of many with mental illness and have been viewed as predictors of relapse—and even the cause of the illness. The social support networks of affected individuals have been the focus of study; the buttressing or creation of such networks has been seen as a viable intervention. In most cases the exploration of these networks involves a review of the number of associates a person has, the density of the network, the relative strength of the ties among people, the general reciprocity among members, and the nature of the support offered. Therefore, most of the analysis centers on the people or groups with whom the individual is involved. Certainly, religious participation involves a connection, or at least contact with, other individuals and perhaps a symbolic tie with a congregation. Beyond this, however, spirituality offers social support that comes from less tangible sources.

From a more traditional view of social support, it is clear that for many with mental illness the church and the congregation provide a consistent haven of support. Clearly, this is not universal, as many encounter the same stigma and rejection in a religious organization as they might in any other social institution—and this was noted by some. However, efforts to create more helpful ties between mental health programs and religious institutions have re-emerged as a point of emphasis in psychosocial rehabilitation. Walters and Neugeboren (1995) observe, "When people who have suffered from long-term mental illness reach the point where they are ready to re-enter the community, church-based programs can become a means to re-enter the normal community, remove the stigma and burdens of being a 'mental patient,' and find socialization and networking opportunities leading to client empowerment and normalization" (p. 52).

Speaking about the support received from their congregation, one informant noted that "they support you and always ask for prayer requests and things like that . . . and they know about my mental illness." The support a congregation offers may also be in the form of more tangible assistance such as clothing, money, invitations to dinner, and the like. One respondent affirmed the importance of worshiping together but also mentioned that "you get involved (after) those things . . . I just know quite a few people there and they help me out quite a bit."

The total power of spirituality as a component of social support may be lost, however, in a traditional analysis of support networks because the sense of having a relationship with, or benefiting from, the guidance of a higher power may not be captured in standard assessments. Pollner (1989) recognizes that "individuals come to feel that with the support and consent of a divine other they can manage or control life events" (p. 91). Given the impress of serious mental illness, and the social response to these conditions, a common experience among those afflicted is to have little control over their lives. This lack of experienced control involves dimensions as far-reaching as the lack of personal space and the lack of control over thoughts and emotions. For some, the sense of support offered by a divine other came at times of greatest despair: "I knew there was a way out and that God was always watching or taking care of me and that in the end result he had it in control—and so I didn't have to do anything stupid or desperate. . . . I might go to heck but he wasn't going to let me go to the bottom."

The first-person reports from those struggling to deal with mental illness emphasize the pain and suffering these persons endure; they also emphasize the courage it takes not to give up. Again, many point to their spirituality as a great aid: "You can't do it on your own, but you can give it to Him; He can take the burden off your shoulders and make it light." In a similar vein, another respondent noted that "you have someone to depend on. Even when no one else is there, you've got God on your side, or Jesus Christ. You don't have to do it on your own."

Commenting on the vulnerability many people with mental illness experience, one person said that "this world can be a bit frightening when you just think about the reality of it. You just feel like an ant at a picnic. . . it [spirituality] just makes you feel more secure."

Spirituality and the Sense of Coherence

Wing (1980, p. 165) offers a consumer's dream to sum up the experience of schizophrenia.

> In this dream I am lying on a beautiful sunlit beach but my body is in pieces. This fact causes me no concern until I realize the tide is coming in and that I am unable to gather the parts of my dismembered body together and run away. The tide gets closer and just when I am on the point of drowning I wake up screaming in panic. This is to me what schizophrenia feels like; being fragmented in one's personality and constantly afraid that the tide of the illness will completely cover me.

Many of the new techniques and interventions designed to help those with serious mental illness have drawn from cognitive and behavioral traditions. Thus, we have focused on skill building and other normalizing experiences to abet the recovery process. Corin and Lauzon (1992) note that this approach focuses on the "objective dimension of symptoms and deficits, and aim(s) at transforming them from the outside" (p. 267). Yet, a forgotten and important aspect of the experience of, and recovery process from, mental illness involves understanding the meaning of the illness experience for the individual. Estroff (1989) writes eloquently about the impact of schizophrenia on the conception of self, noting that "becoming a schizophrenic is essentially a social and interpersonal process, not an inevitable consequence of primary symptoms and neurochemical abnormality" (p. 194).

Earlier it was suggested that religious institutions may provide opportunities for a gradual return to routine community life. The potential benefits of spirituality and religion are far more complex than simple socialization opportunities. Ventis (1995) argues that involvement with a religious community is to share common beliefs that can serve as central organizing principles in one's personality. Extending this argument further, Idler (1987) proposes that religious participation provides "access to a unique system of symbols, providing cultural resources in the form of a consistent body of knowledge and set of meanings that allow individuals to make sense of and cope with their experience, reducing uncertainty in ordinary life and at moments of crisis alike" (p. 229).

For some of the respondents in this study, it is clear that spirituality and religious involvement have been important parts of their lives since childhood, although some speak of losing their faith for a time while they were ill. Walsh (1995) believes that a person's religious disposition tends to persist despite the onset of schizophrenia. Furthermore, interpersonal connections can suffer due to the illness, but religion allows one "to identify with a community that transcends self" (Walsh, 1995, p. 553). Turning to one's beliefs in a time of crisis in such cases is a natural way of handling life's difficulties. It is here that one sees an unwavering belief that spirituality is central to these individuals' recovery: "I believe in prayer and I believe in the faith of God, and so I believe those prayers are answered by God." Most important, perhaps, is the simple affirmation that spirituality is an important part of their lives: "It's a big deal for me. It helps me to be a whole person, and it's not going to take, or rid you of paranoid thoughts necessarily, but it will help you cope with them."

Discussion and Implications

The study recounted here, as well as in other first-person reports, indicates that religion and spirituality are viewed by former and current consumers of mental health services as important to their recovery. That spirituality would be central to many who have mental illness should not be surprising, given the importance that many people in all life circumstances ascribe to this aspect of their lives. It is equally clear from these informants that religious preoccupation can be harmful and, at times, lead to delusional thoughts and irrational behavior.

This study underscores the fact that the recovery process cannot be measured simply by outward behavior and activities alone but is a process with internal and personal dimensions. Thus, hope, confidence, a strong sense of will, and other less tangible aspects of a person's character are also keys to recovery. This further suggests that the relationship between the helper and the consumer is still vitally important.

Because recovery has an internal dimension, the process may actually begin long before professionals note any appreciable progress, or even when they are most concerned about consumers. Corin and Lauzon (1992) introduced the concept of *positive withdrawal,* observing that "what can be perceived from the outside as a negative feature, indicative of passivity and deterioration, can be an important part of a larger restructuring process" (p. 272). Positive withdrawal can be characterized as a period when the individual engages in a process of making sense of the self and illness while mustering the courage to confront the demands of the external world. Corin and Lauzon (1992) note that "the use of religious signifiers emerges as a privileged way of reframing a withdrawn position within a meaningful context" (p. 276). Here, withdrawal becomes synonymous with a solitary or meditative retreat.

Accepting the proposition that religion and spirituality are important to the recovery process for those with serious mental illness still leaves professionals with questions about how to use this knowledge in their work. Little controversy surrounds the idea that establishing relationships with churches and congregations who may be in a good position to be of help to consumers is useful (Walters and Neugeboren, 1995). Churches are like many social resources that can benefit the reintegration of consumers, particularly when the clergy and congregation are knowledgeable about mental illness.

A far more complicated issue is the desirability of professionals directly working with consumers around issues of religion and spirituality. Many professionals are uncomfortable with the issues, or they feel that dealing with such issues is inappropriate. Additionally, while some consumers express an interest in exploring spiritual issues in therapy, others clearly do not (Lindgren and Coursey, 1995). Reviewing the results of their study, Lindgren and Coursey (1995) conclude that although a discussion of spiritual concerns can be of therapeutic value, such a discussion should proceed cautiously.

Conclusion

It has been argued here that religion and spirituality are important ingredients in the recovery process for many who have mental illness. This conclusion has been drawn, not from any preconceived notions about the power of faith and belief but from research and first-person accounts. It has also been argued that those helping consumers in the recovery process must first listen actively and learn from those consumers.

References

Allport, G. W. "Behavioral Science, Religion, and Mental Health." *Journal of Religion and Health,* 1963, 2 (3), 187–197.

Anthony, W. A. "Recovery from Mental Illness: The Guiding Vision of the Mental Health Service System in the 1990s." *Psychosocial Rehabilitation Journal,* 1993, 16 (4), 11–23.

Cooper, E. "To Be Rooted." *The Journal of the California Alliance for the Mentally Ill,* 1993, 3 (4), 15–16.

Corin, E., and Lauzon, G. "Positive Withdrawal and the Quest for Meaning: The Reconstruction of Experience among Schizophrenics." *Psychiatry,* 1992, 55, 266–278.

Dull, V., and Skokan, L. "A Cognitive Model of Religion's Influence on Health." *Journal of Social Issues,* 1995, 51 (2), 49–64.

Ellison, C. "Religious Involvement and Subjective Well-Being." *Journal of Health and Social Behavior,* 1991, 31 (1), 80–99.

Estroff, S. "Self, Identity, and Subjective Experiences of Schizophrenia: In Search of the Subject." *Schizophrenia Bulletin,* 1989, 15 (2), 189–196.

Estroff, S. "Commentary on Corin and Lauzon." *Psychiatry,* 1992, 55, 279–281.

Estroff, S. "Keeping Things Complicated: Undiscovered Countries and the Lives of Persons with Serious Mental Illness." *The Journal of California Alliance for the Mentally Ill,* 1994, 5 (3), 40–46.

Giglio, J. "The Impact of Patients' and Therapists' Religious Values on Psychotherapy." *Hospital and Community Psychiatry,* 1993, 44 (8), 768–771.

Harding, C., Zubin, J., and Strauss, J. "Chronicity in Schizophrenia: Revisited." *British Journal of Psychiatry*, 1992, *161*, 27–37.

Hathaway, W., and Pargament, K. "Intrinsic Religiousness, Religious Coping, and Psychosocial Competence: A Covariance Structure Analysis." *Journal for the Scientific Study of Religion*, 1990, *29* (4), 423–441.

Idler, E. "Religious Involvement and the Health of the Elderly: Some Hypotheses and an Initial Test." *Social Forces*, 1987, *66* (1), 226–238.

Kleinman, A. *The Illness Narratives*. New York: Basic Books, 1988.

Lindgren, K., and Coursey, R. "Spirituality and Serious Mental Illness: A Two-Part Study." *Psychosocial Rehabilitation Journal*, 1995, *18* (3), 93–111.

Maton, K. "The Stress-Buffering Role of Spiritual Support: Cross-Sectional and Prospective Investigations." *Journal for the Scientific Study of Religion*, 1989, *28* (3), 310–323.

Michello, J. "Spiritual and Emotional Determinants of Health." *Journal of Religion and Health*, 1988, *27* (1), 62–70.

Pargament, K., Ensing, D., Falgout, K., Olsen, H., Reilly, B., Van Haitsma, K., and Warren, W. "God Help Me: Religious Coping Efforts as Predictors of the Outcome to Significant Negative Life Events." *American Journal of Community Psychology*, 1990, *18* (6), 793–824.

Petersen, L., and Roy, A. "Religiosity, Anxiety, and Meaning and Purpose: Religion's Consequences for Psychological Well-Being." *Review of Religious Research*, 1985, *27* (1), 49–62.

Pollner, M. "Divine Relations, Social Relations, and Well-Being." *Journal of Health and Social Behavior*, 1989, *30*, 92–104.

Spradley, J. *The Ethnographic Interview*. New York: Holt, Rinehart and Winston, 1979.

Sullivan, W. P. "Spirituality as Social Support for Individuals with Severe Mental Illness." *Spirituality and Social Work Journal*, 1992, *3* (1), 7–13.

Sullivan, W. P. "Recovery from Schizophrenia: What We can Learn from the Developing Nations." *Innovations and Research*, 1994a, *3* (2), 7–15.

Sullivan, W. P. "A Long and Winding Road: The Process of Recovery from Mental Illness." *Innovations and Research*, 1994, *3* (3), 19–27.

Titone, A. "Spirituality and Psychotherapy in Social Work Practice." *Spirituality and Social Work Communicator*, 1991, *2* (1), 7–9.

Ventis, W. L. "The Relationships Between Religion and Mental Health." *Journal of Social Issues*, 1995, *51* (2), 33–48.

Walsh, J. "The Impact of Schizophrenia on Clients' Religious Beliefs: Implications for Families." *Families in Society*, 1995, *76* (9), 551–558.

Walters, J., and Neugeboren, B. "Collaboration Between Mental Health Organizations and Religious Institutions." *Psychiatric Rehabilitation Journal*, 1995, *19* (2), 51–57.

Wing, J. "Schizophrenia from Within." In H. Rollin (ed.), *Coping with Schizophrenia*. London: Burnett Books, 1980.

W. PATRICK SULLIVAN *is associate professor of social work, Indiana University School of Social Work, Indianapolis.*

Key themes in narratives of recovery from mental illness illustrate some of the functions of religion and spirituality in consumers' self-understanding and coping.

Spiritual and Religious Dimensions of Mental Illness Recovery Narratives

Roger D. Fallot

Theorists in many fields of inquiry have examined the importance of narrative in structuring human experience. Philosophers of religion (Crites, 1971), theologians (Goldberg, 1982), personality theorists (McAdams, 1993), psychoanalysts (Spence, 1982; Schafer, 1983), and psychiatric rehabilitation specialists (Harris and others, 1997), among others, have demonstrated the many ways in which stories may provide coherence, meaning, and direction to self-understanding. McAdams (1993) claims that each of us "naturally constructs [a story] to bring together the different parts of ourselves and our lives into a purposeful and convincing whole" (p. 13). In the last decade, this line of thinking has come to include the stories people tell of their experiences with illness and suffering: their "illness narratives" (Kleinman, 1988; Frank, 1995). Focusing on the spiritual and religious dimensions of stories, this chapter explores a narrative approach to the experiences of people who have been diagnosed with severe mental illness and discusses the roles such stories may play in recovery.

The stories people tell about their lives call attention to the need to make sense of—to discover or construct meaning in response to—life events and circumstances. Personal narratives have the power not only to disclose the individual's core values and implicit philosophies but to shape ongoing life activities—to open up some possibilities and to constrict others. For instance, if a particular story, overtly or covertly, prioritizes constancy and minimizes change, the individual's motivation for maintaining stability may be paramount, and exploring alternatives may be correspondingly foreshortened.

Like all stories, personal narratives may be viewed through the lens of literary criticism. Theme, plot and subplot, characterization, activity, tone, movement, and voice are among the listener's descriptive and interpretive tools. Frank (1995), writing primarily about chronic physical illnesses, offers a typology of illness narratives. *Restitution* narratives, he claims, convey a central movement motif—from a state of health through one of illness to restored well-being. In distinct contrast, *chaos* narratives lack clear, linear movement. They are more reactive to momentary stress than they are reflective; they hold little hope that life will get better. Finally, Frank notes, is the *quest* narrative—the type most commonly seen in published illness stories. Here the teller accepts the illness and holds to the belief that something may be gained through its experience. The illness becomes the occasion for discovering and enacting some purpose on the quest.

Led by consumers, the mental health field has come, in the last decade, to place increasing emphasis on the concept of recovery (Anthony, 1993; Spaniol, Koehler, and Hutchinson, 1994). In fact, many of the writings by consumers (Cooke, 1997; Deegan, 1988; Unzicker, 1989) spurring this new emphasis may be thought of as *recovery narratives*. By this I mean that writers often frame their personal stories of mental illness, its impact, and its aftermath in recovery terms; they acknowledge both the reality of mental illness and its effects, yet develop a sense of meaning and direction that supports their moving beyond the limitations imposed by the illness and by societal responses to it. Recovery, in this context, involves narrative themes of challenge and hope, of stigma and assertiveness, of limitations and new possibilities, of struggle and empowerment.

Published recovery narratives in mental illness have drawn primarily, then, on elements of Frank's quest narratives, whereas restitution and times of acknowledged chaos are secondary. The reality of most persistent and recurring mental illnesses is a cyclical one that "complicates enormously the problem of establishing new identities, new purposes, and new meanings" (Hatfield and Lefley, 1993, p. 186), as well as new personal narratives. When the very illness around which recovery is sought may function to disturb mood or to cloud cognitive clarity, the process of consistent meaning-making is itself at risk. So it becomes all the more important for many consumers to weave a self-story encompassing disruption, stability, and growth.

From this perspective, mental illness recovery narratives reflect a particular set of values and related motifs that place the individual in relationship to her or his immediate and larger contexts. They provide a general orienting system in which specific coping techniques may find particular salience. Because of this overarching function of recovery narratives, religious and spiritual themes may be of great importance for many individuals. Spiritual commitments may dispose people to make sense of their experience in ways consistent with their religious beliefs, to draw on religious resources for both more general and more specific coping (Pargament, 1997), and to construct further narrative developments so that they take spiritual realities into consideration. So, although recovery narratives may serve as coping mechanisms for dealing with the stressors related to mental illness, they do so primarily by offering a more comprehensive scheme for understanding, adapting to, and overcoming the challenges of severe mental disorders—a scheme that for many individuals includes religious and spiritual dimensions.

This is not to say, of course, that spirituality always plays a positive role in these narratives and in their associated coping styles. As noted in the introductory chapter to this volume, religious and spiritual concerns may become part of the problem as well as part of the recovery. Some people have experienced organized religion, for example, as a source of pain or guilt or oppression. Rather than being a positive resource for recovery, religion in this sense may merely deepen and complicate the need for recovery. Alongside those who experience the faith community as welcoming and hospitable are those who find it stigmatizing and rejecting. Alongside those who feel uplifted by spiritual activities are those who feel burdened by them. And alongside those who find comfort and strength in religiousness are those who find disappointment and demoralization. Given the relative neglect of religious issues in the mental health field, however, and given a history of overemphasis on the difficulties associated with religion, it is important to see that for many people with severe mental illnesses, spirituality is a core element in the narrative context for recovery.

Key Religious and Spiritual Themes in Recovery Narratives

In spiritual discussion groups, psychotherapy sessions, consumer satisfaction interviews, trauma recovery groups, clinical interviews, and numerous consultations at Community Connections, individuals have shared parts of their personal recovery stories. Before turning to certain themes distilled from these interactions, it is important to indicate some of the characteristics of these consumers. Consumers at Community Connections have all been diagnosed with a severe mental illness at one time. They are predominantly African American and largely identify themselves as Christians, mostly Protestant. Significant histories of substance abuse, physical and sexual abuse, homelessness, and poverty are also prevalent in this inner-city population. Recovery in this setting is thus not focused only on the experience of mental illness but is a multidimensional process that responds to broadly based experiences of marginalization and victimization.

Theme One: Whole-Person Recovery Takes Whole-Person Involvement. For many people, recovery narratives may draw on a somewhat paradoxical image of spirituality: it is at once the most profound center of one's life and the most encompassing whole. In a survey at Community Connections, nearly half of the participants agreed or strongly agreed with this statement: "My whole approach to life is based on my religion" (Fallot and Azrin, 1995). This sort of affirmation—that spirituality lies at the heart of recovery and that it forms the basis for other dimensions of growth—is common. It may be rooted in the beliefs and rituals of organized religion, in twelve-step programs that emphasize the centrality of a higher power, or in a personal conviction that the self is most clearly defined by its spiritual expression. But whatever its foundation, *spirituality* as the core of identity stands as a sharp contrast and frequent antidote to *mental illness* as a core identity. People who incorporate in their recovery stories an understanding of themselves as children of God or as being an integral part of the larger world often adopt a more positive and hopeful tone about their place and roles in the community.

When consumers say, then, that "spirituality has been the most important part of my recovery," they are often referring to this whole-person orientation. Usually such comments are not intended to minimize the value of psychiatric medications nor of psychotherapeutic relationships nor of other rehabilitative supports. But they do claim a holism that points beyond the biopsychosocial dimensions to an ultimate source of meaning and identity.

Theme Two: True Recovery Is a Long-Term and Often Effortful Journey. Many religious traditions and spiritual movements offer avenues to healing. The image of spiritual growth as a journey or pilgrimage is a prominent one. Recovery narratives drawing on this theme differ significantly from those calling for a quick and all-encompassing solution to the problems attending mental illness. One spiritual discussion group, for instance, explored the distinctions between *magic* and *healing*. Some individuals held out hope for a "magic pill" or life-transforming moment that would relieve them of their struggles, whereas others talked about their own experiences with healing and recovery as a journey that requires considerable time and effort. The latter group strongly opposed the notion that some human or divine intervention would instantly change their lives. Rather, they emphasized their own responsibility and activity while simultaneously drawing on the sustenance of divine support. This stance, they claimed, led to greater fulfillment and less disappointment than passively waiting for miracles.

Theme Three: Hope Is an Essential Ingredient for Continuing Recovery. The recurrent nature of most severe mental disorders is often demoralizing for consumers, families, friends, and professionals. Given such cyclical problems, the maintenance of a hopeful position is difficult. Yet, according to many consumers, it is also essential to sustained recovery. Spirituality and religion are prime resources for hope. Some consumers build hopeful elements of their recovery narratives around beliefs in God and God's benevolence ("God's purposes are for the best" or "God will never give me more than I can handle" or "God wants the best for my life"). Christians reported drawing on scriptural stories of hope in the face of apparently overwhelming obstacles (the account of God's deliverance of the Hebrew people from Egypt, for example). The idea of a force in the universe that is allied with good and opposed to evil was voiced by some individuals who did not see themselves as connected to organized religion. Being in tune with this positive power then became a reason for hopefulness.

Many recovery narratives struggle with the difference between realistic hope and blind optimism. More realistically hopeful stories acknowledge the difficulties posed by mental illness and by societal responses to it but find hope in spite of these problems. Other narratives minimize or deny them, asserting that all will somehow work out for the best. Spiritual and religious dimensions of hope, then, place it in its ultimate context of divine or universal purposes. Personal narratives may draw on this ultimacy to sustain hope necessary for the journey.

Theme Four: Recovery Depends on the Experience of Loving Relationships. Many stories include the importance of divine love in strengthening and sustaining recovery. This experience of relationship with God, often nurtured in religious practice, may have affirming and valuing motifs—that God truly cares for each person as an individual and that God is deeply interested in each person's welfare. When a personal God-image is less prominent, a sacred quality of love may still be acknowledged. Some research has supported the idea that relationships with "divine others" may be related to psychological aspects of well-being (Pollner, 1989). In qualitative terms, stories that describe the self as strengthened by this relationship seem to involve greater confidence, capacity to tolerate stress, and willingness to take initiative. One woman talked about how her relationship with God had given her inner strength so that she could face more directly the pain of her trauma history and mental illness.

Some recovery narratives give a prominent place to reciprocal caring; one must give as well as receive love in order to feel whole. One man described his struggles, for example, with the idea of loving your enemies. This was hardly an abstract concern for him, as it directly affected how he chose to handle conflicts with roommates and other acquaintances. How tolerant or how confrontational should he be? Other people recounted the vitalizing importance of caring for their children. Especially when such care had been disrupted by psychiatric or substance abuse problems, recovery of these connections focused not simply on renewed contact with their children but on re-establishing ongoing loving relationships. For many consumers, the love found in human relationships is a reflection of the sacred—a further expression of divine love. For others, it is a primary animating force, giving direction and purpose to daily life.

Theme Five: The "Serenity Prayer" Expresses a Key Process in Recovery. It is perhaps not surprising in a population with extensive substance abuse and twelve-step experience that Reinhold Niebuhr's ([1943] 1980) "Serenity Prayer" should have a prominent place in many recovery narratives: "God, give us grace to accept with serenity the things that cannot be changed, courage to change the things which should be changed, and the wisdom to distinguish the one from the other" (p. 823). Yet the images involved in this prayer are by no means limited in applicability to those with addictive disorders. When applied to coping with the apparent vagaries of mental illness, disability, societal stigma, and discrimination, such wisdom is indeed highly valued. Many consumers have built some version of this sentiment into their spiritual understanding and practice. Each phrase has a unique part to play in recovery.

Simply deciding which goal to pursue or which problem to address is daunting for many individuals with mental disorders. Choosing to focus on those over which the individual has or can develop greater control is often portrayed as a key step in recovery. Having devoted too much effort to attempts to change other people or to meet unrealistic expectations or to conquer psychiatric symptoms by using will power, consumers here describe the tremendous relief, hopefulness, and confidence that may grow from identifying goals over which they can exert at least some significant control. Rather than feeling aimless in their recovery attempts, they feel an enhanced ability to channel energy toward arenas in which their efforts are likely to make a difference. So the "wisdom to know the difference" is often recognized as a turning point in recovery stories.

Second, many consumers recount their attempts to accept aspects of their lives that cannot be changed. Most commonly, the stories of their personal, sometimes painful, pasts pose special challenges in this regard. Some expressions capture specific, religiously framed variations of this process: "Letting go and letting God" or "I turned that over [to God]" or "I left that in God's hands." Others rely on twelve-step acknowledgments of powerlessness and reliance on a higher power than the self. There may be struggles around the apparent intractability of the consumer's problems. In some recovery narratives, the ability to accept periodic symptoms without accepting the demoralizing idea of being chronically and permanently disabled led to significantly greater motivation. Recognizing that the acknowledgment of their mental illness did not require them to renounce meaningful life goals was in fact energizing rather than depleting.

Finally, the "courage to change the things I can" takes on special significance in many recovery stories. The importance of developing assertiveness and the experience of empowerment can hardly be overstated in this context. Empowerment is both the central value and central goal of the recovery movement for many consumers. Developing or renewing a sense of power in solving personal problems and pursuing meaningful life goals is a corollary of this principle. Mental illness recovery stories often highlight learnings around symptom management, including the importance of medication, ways to minimize intrusive thoughts or hallucinations, and methods for coping with identified stressors. Developing and enhancing skills in interpersonal, educational, or vocational domains contribute to a sense of empowerment, as does the ability to define one's own needs and hopes and actively seek to fulfill them. Consumers report that having a more effective voice and becoming an active collaborator in their own service planning and evaluation is often one of the main shifts toward greater personal strength. Many understand this empowerment in terms that reflect spiritual or religious convictions in addition to any psychosocial ones. The divine or sacred can be a resounding source of personal power, which can be expressed as follows: being uplifted or given courage, feeling valued enough not to settle for less than one deserves, being freed to follow one's own life course, and cultivating the belief that God wants each person to live a life of abundant wholeness.

Yet empowerment to change what can be changed may include not only immediate personal and interpersonal spheres but public and political ones as well. Although for many consumers this is a secularly informed concern, for many others it has distinctly religious and spiritual meanings. Some consumers talk of their involvement in advocacy or in public policy (as well as in personal choices) as a *mission* or a *vocation*. Both of these terms may carry traditional religious implications. The consumer's story is being allied with a larger sacred story, and his or her purpose is being allied with larger, often divinely construed, purposes. This is precisely where some mental health professionals become skeptical about the use of religious language. For example, does talking about "doing God's will" necessarily point to some delusional process? Only a careful assessment of the meaning of such language—both in that individual's overall functioning and in any relevant faith community context—can provide answers to this question. But for many people with severe mental illnesses, such a claim does not differ from that made in spiritual or religious contexts by innumerable believers. Their faith entails developing a sense of their unique role (a calling, perhaps) in bringing into reality certain core values.

It is certainly true that for some individuals the "Serenity Prayer" is useful primarily as a cognitive-behavioral framing; it serves to distinguish the controllable from the inevitable and to focus change efforts in the most potentially responsive arenas. For many others, however, the fact that it is offered as a prayer is essential to its power. Its petitionary form places the serenity, courage, and wisdom sought in the context of the individual's relationship with God (and often that of a faith community as well). For believers, this is especially relevant. Bringing such fundamental requests to God acknowledges in process what is stated in content: that these virtues may not be entirely at the individual's disposal and that they may be more properly experienced as gifts than as achievements.

Theme Six: Recovery Is a Journey Toward Genuineness and Authenticity. One of Frank's (1995) primary interpretive categories for illness narratives is the extent to which the teller's unique voice finds clear expression. In the accounts of people recovering from mental illness, this experience is also central and often enormously complex. Many metaphors reflect this process: discovering—or rediscovering—one's "true self"; feeling that one is "centered" or "grounded"; recognizing moments when action emerges from what is "really me" or truly "spontaneous"; becoming more regularly in consonance with "who I really am." Some frame this as a journey of return; its imagery involves "getting back to the person I was" (usually before the trauma or substance abuse or symptoms of mental illness) and thus draws on restitution themes. Some view it as a journey forward; the emerging self is being both discovered and created along the way, incorporating many struggles as well as achievements in its composition. Although consumers in either case often report the challenges of recognizing and consolidating a consistent sense of self in light of complicating psychiatric symptoms, there remains a fundamental motive to do so.

In some frameworks, the development of greater authenticity is inherently and implicitly a spiritual concern. Nothing is more fundamental to human existence than the achievement of genuine selfhood. In others, this connection to the spiritual or religious is explicit. Being "the self that one is meant to be" points to a sense of ultimacy, of underlying direction and coherence that transcends that self. Many religious people place this ultimacy in relationship to a personal God or to a faith community in which one's genuine identity is formed and finds fulfillment. Many recovery stories place authentic self-expression, then, in the context of spiritual and religious life. Here the "true self" emerges not only in dialogue with one's own history and one's own relational context but with the most basic questions of identity, meaning, and purpose.

Theme Seven: Recovery Is a Story of Action and Pragmatism as Well as Conviction. Many of the previous themes have emphasized the kinds of understandings and beliefs that characterize spirituality in recovery narratives of people with mental illness. But virtually all of these stories have concrete implications for daily living. Some examples will demonstrate the more immediate functions of these activities.

Faith communities. Religious groups can be a profound source of affirmation, comfort, and belonging in the lives of individuals who have often experienced stigma, rejection, and exclusion. One woman who had returned to church after many years of homelessness and isolation talked about her surprise and gratification that she could once again join others in worship, that she could be accepted—even welcomed—by such a community, and that she could begin to fit in with a group that represented key values in her life. Others describe the ways in which faith communities have extended themselves to meet some specific need—for transportation or food or emotional support. For people whose sense of themselves as marginal and unworthy is frequently reinforced by the larger society, religious groups may play a powerful role in reasserting their value and place in the wider community and in offering social, emotional, and tangible supports.

Prayer and meditation. Meditative time may deepen a sense of connection to self and, in prayer, to God. But mental illness recovery narratives often recount other, more tangible benefits as well. Some stories emphasize prayer or meditation as a very specific mode of self-soothing—a calming, relaxing, and reassuring response to external or internal stress, including hallucinations. Others focus more on its problem-solving functions: talking things over with God helps to sort through options and make better decisions; prayer reinforces motivation for abstinence from drugs and alcohol; meditating or praying puts things back in perspective and helps control emotional over-reaction. Still others describe how prayer improves mood. It may renew hope and expand the range of personal possibilities, or it may cultivate a sense of gratitude and draw attention to the positive aspects of some individuals' lives, or it may clarify a sense of purpose. Whether one considers their more abstract or more concrete effects, prayer and meditation often play an active role in these recovery narratives.

Religious literature and music. Both devotional materials and scripture appear frequently in the stories of people recovering from mental illness. Over half of the Community Connections participants in a recent survey said that they read scripture at least once a month (Fallot and Azrin, 1995). In addition to the general deepening of spiritual life this literature offers, it may also be responsive to specific individual needs. For example, certain biblical passages (such as many of the Psalms) are deeply reassuring and comforting. They may be read repeatedly as a steady source of strength or may be drawn on in particular moments of stress. Other passages speak directly to God's concern for the sick and the marginalized and serve as distinct reminders of God's care. Consumers read still others as challenges to use all of their talents and strengths as fully as possible.

Listening to religious music has in some ways very similar functions in recovery stories: comforting, strengthening, reminding, and challenging. African American spirituals, for instance, have special significance for many believers. This music expresses a wide and deep emotional range, engaging listeners in both the painful reality of suffering and the comfort, hope, and joy available to the faithful. And actively participating in the singing and movement of religious music may offer social and emotional benefits beyond that of listening. A gospel music group at Community Connections has played an important role for people (re)discovering musical interests and abilities. It has encouraged many people who are usually withdrawn and isolated to join in making music and in sharing their talents publicly. Culturally as well as musically, singing has helped many group members re-establish active roles in an important community.

Ritual. For many people with severe mental illness, disorganization has characterized a great deal of their daily lives. It is not surprising, then, that rituals associated with religion or spirituality are highly valued by consumers who prize their structure, regularity, and predictability. Whether these are rituals built around personal practice (for example, prayer at regular times, devotional readings, listening to music, watching worship services on television) or they constitute participation in formally structured activities of a faith community (worship, community service, making music), many recovery narratives describe the important capacity of such rituals to organize experience, provide meaning, offer trustworthy and safe social engagement, and express core beliefs.

Conclusion

These themes are intended to be an illustrative rather than exhaustive compilation of the ways spirituality and religion may serve as resources in the stories people tell of their ongoing recovery from mental illness. Such stories present important opportunities for mental health professionals working with this group of people. First, service providers may serve as accepting and empathic hearers of these stories, including their religious and spiritual dimensions. Rather than ignoring or minimizing references to spirituality in recovery and rehabilitation, these domains should be explored seriously. And, if an assessment supports the value of religion in a particular consumer's recovery, clinicians should be prepared to support collaboratively the consumer's convictions and practices. Second, professionals may play a very important role in the further development and elaboration of recovery narratives. Recovery stories do not emerge in a vacuum. They are created out of the teller's relationships and conversations with important others and from available social and cultural resources. By actively engaging with the consumer's story, the clinician offers new perspectives, challenges limits, and affirms strengths. Being respectfully open to expression of spiritual beliefs and activities is one of the keys to facilitating the telling and living of many consumers' recovery stories.

References

Anthony, W. A. "Recovery from Mental Illness: The Guiding Vision of the Mental Health Service System in the 1990s." *Psychosocial Rehabilitation Journal,* 1993, *16* (4), 11–23.

Cooke, A. M. "The Long Journey Back." *Psychiatric Rehabilitation Skills,* 1997, *2* (1), 33–36.

Crites, S. "The Narrative Quality of Experience." *Journal of the American Academy of Religion,* 1971, *39,* 291–311.

Deegan, P. E. "Recovery: The Lived Experience of Rehabilitation." *Psychosocial Rehabilitation Journal,* 1988, *11* (4), 11–19.

Fallot, R. D., and Azrin, S. T. "Consumer Satisfaction: Findings from a Case Management Program Evaluation Study." Paper presented at the Annual Conference of the International Association of Psychosocial Rehabilitation Services, Boston, June 1995.

Frank, A. W. *The Wounded Storyteller: Body, Illness, and Ethics.* Chicago: University of Chicago Press, 1995.

Goldberg, M. *Theology and Narrative.* Nashville: Abingdon Press, 1982.

Harris, M., Bebout, R. R., Freeman, D. W., Hobbs, M. D., Kline, J. D., Miller, S. L., and Vanasse, L. D. "Work Stories: Psychological Responses to Work in a Population of Dually Diagnosed Adults." *Psychiatric Quarterly,* 1997, *68* (2), 131–153.

Hatfield, A. B., and Lefley, H. P. *Surviving Mental Illness: Stress, Coping, and Adaptation.* New York: Guilford Press, 1993.

Kleinman, A. *The Illness Narratives: Suffering, Healing, and the Human Condition.* New York: Basic Books, 1988.

McAdams, D. P. *Stories We Live By: Personal Myths and the Making of the Self.* New York: Morrow, 1993.

Niebuhr, R. "The Serenity Prayer." In E. M. Beck (ed.), *Bartlett's Familiar Quotations.* (15th ed.) Boston: Little, Brown, 1980.

Pargament, K. I. *The Psychology of Religion and Coping: Theory, Research, and Practice.* New York: Guilford Press, 1997.

Pollner, M. "Divine Relations, Social Relations, and Well-Being." *Journal of Health and Social Behavior,* 1989, *30,* 92–104.

Schafer, R. *The Analytic Attitude.* New York: Basic Books, 1983.

Spaniol, L., Koehler, M., and Hutchinson, D. *The Recovery Workbook: Practical Coping and Empowerment Strategies for People with Psychiatric Disability.* Boston: Center for Psychiatric Rehabilitation, 1994.

Spence, D. P. *Narrative Truth and Historical Truth: Meaning and Interpretation in Psychoanalysis.* New York: Norton, 1982.

Unzicker, R. "On My Own: A Personal Journey through Madness and Re-emergence." *Psychosocial Rehabilitation Journal,* 1989, *13* (1), 71–77.

ROGER D. FALLOT is co-director of Community Connections in Washington, D.C., and a member of the adjunct faculty in pastoral counseling at Loyola College in Maryland.

*The long-standing success of a Spiritual Beliefs and Values Group
supports the potential value of discussing spiritual issues and
challenges the assumption that religious concerns voiced by people with
serious mental illness should be considered pathological.*

Religious-Issues Group Therapy

Nancy C. Kehoe

Will the discussion of religion and spirituality with seriously mentally ill individuals cause more problems than it solves? Will such a discussion support a person's delusions, strengthen his or her defenses, encourage immaturity, aid in avoidance of responsibility, foster dogmatism, and promote unhealthy dependence? To answer these questions, I report on clinical evidence gathered from sixteen years of religious-issues group therapy. The thesis of this chapter is that men and women diagnosed with major mental illness are not harmed by discussing religion and spirituality but, in fact, are helped by it.

Religious-Issues Groups in the Published Literature

Although there is an extensive body of literature on serious mental illness and religion, and much literature on groups, a comprehensive computer search revealed few studies of groups focusing on religious beliefs for people with severe mental disorders.

Worthington, Kurusu, and McCullough (1996) reviewed the published empirical studies and the reviews of empirical research on religion and psychotherapeutic processes and outcomes. They found that community interventions have neither been proposed nor investigated and that religiously oriented group therapy or psychoeducational groups have been underinvestigated, despite the active use of groups in treatment programs. Gartner, Larson, and Allens' (1991) review reports no literature involving group work focused on religious beliefs.

Although several articles have supported the importance of spirituality in the lives of people with mental illness, few of these have addressed the value of group work. Sullivan (1993) interviewed about forty adults who, at some point in their lives, had been diagnosed with a serious mental illness. The purpose of the interview was to discern factors that could account for the interviewees' current successful functioning in the community; 48 percent mentioned spiritual beliefs or practices as central to their success. Kroll and Sheehan (1989) studied the religious beliefs and practices among fifty-two psychiatric inpatients in Minnesota and noted that "the religious life of psychiatric patients has rarely been either the subject of or an important variable in psychiatric studies" (p. 67). They note, "Religious beliefs and practices take an important and often central place in the lives of many of our patients" (p. 71).

In order to cope with major stressors such as mental illness, individuals bring with them a system of beliefs, practices, aspirations, and relationships that affects how they deal with such difficulties. Religion, according to Pargament and others (1992), is to a greater or lesser extent a part of a person's general orienting system. Neither Pargament nor Kroll, however, has looked at this inquiry in relation to group work with individuals who have a mental illness.

Only two articles were found that specifically address the discussion of religious beliefs in groups of people with serious mental illness. Lindgren and Coursey (1995) conducted a highly structured, four-week psychoeducational program with clients who were in psychosocial rehabilitation centers and were interested in spirituality. The goal of the program was to help clients utilize their spiritual beliefs to foster healthy self-esteem. The design included both an experimental group and a wait-list control group, as well as interviews with all who had initially volunteered to participate. There was a significant change in the Spiritual Support Scale from pretest to posttest for those who had been a part of the intervention. However, a second analysis compared those who had participated in the intervention to those who did not and found no significant differences on measures of depression, hopelessness, self-esteem, or purpose in life (a finding the authors thought may be due to the low power of the second analysis). The authors acknowledge several limitations of their study: its small sample size, the time-limited intervention, and the fact that those who volunteered were interested in the topic of spirituality. Their findings, though, suggest that one aspect of spirituality or religion—providing people with cognitive mediation or emotional support—helps individuals who have serious mental illness, as it does those who have serious physical illness (Byrd, 1988; Levin, 1989; Matthews, Larson, and Barry, 1993; Koenig, 1997).

O'Rourke (1997), using the group model created by this author, found that the Spiritual Issues Group provided clients with a "transitional space to work through developmental and emotional issues," which fostered a sense of higher functioning and object constancy. The group described by Genia (1990), although similar in content and format to the group that is the subject of this chapter, did not include clients with serious mental illness.

Purpose of the Present Study

In this chapter, I describe my sixteen-year experience of leading groups on the topic, "Spiritual Beliefs and Values," with men and women who have serious mental illness. This experience illustrates the ways in which individuals can examine their beliefs, recognize the potential for delusion, distinguish what appears to be helpful from what is problematic about their beliefs, and develop both tolerance and understanding for religious or spiritual differences. The author describes the groups, examines what has occurred in the course of the sixteen-year study period, and provides examples from group sessions as illustrations. (Although the term *group* will be used in the singular, the experience of multiple groups with changing membership actually forms the basis for this chapter.)

The first group began when staff at a day treatment program requested a consultation because a therapist and a client were at an impasse over religious issues. Following the consultation, the staff identified many other clients for whom religion seemed to be important. No one, however, knew how to deal with the religious material. The consultant's suggestion that a group be organized to focus on religious issues was ultimately accepted but not without considerable staff anxiety. The very idea—having a group on religious issues for men and women with serious mental illness—generated fear and doubt. The idea touched some of the staff's own ambivalence about religion and spirituality. They raised the following questions: Would the clients become *more* delusional? Would they try to split the staff on religious issues? Would they use the group to avoid other therapeutic work? Would they use their beliefs as an escape or as a way to rationalize their current situation? Would the group members be able to tolerate the sectarian differences among them? What would be the interaction between their illness, their treatment, and their religious or spiritual beliefs?

No one knew the answers to these questions, but the questions themselves suggested a negative bias toward religion and spirituality and toward clients' abilities to discuss these issues. The relationship between a person's beliefs and his or her illness is complex; however, empirical evidence shows that even people with serious mental illness can discuss, explore, and search for understanding about their faith and their psychic health or illness.

Goals of the Religious-Issues Group

The primary goals of the religious-issues group are to provide a therapeutic context for clients' examination of their religious beliefs, their religious traditions, and their family's involvement in a religious tradition, as well as to facilitate the exploration of some of the questions, problems, and feelings clients have about their religious beliefs, their spiritual beliefs, or the absence of either in their lives. The group also offers an opportunity to explore the ways in which religious or spiritual beliefs and values are, or are not, a part of clients' lives.

The goal of the group is neither to present different didactic models of religion and spirituality nor to suggest ways that religion or spirituality might be useful to clients (as the Lindgren and Coursey study did). Nor is the superiority of one belief over another an issue. Instead, the basic ground rule and fundamental value of the group is that each person and his or her beliefs are to be respected. The group is not a prayer group, nor is it a Bible study group; no one is allowed to proselytize.

These guidelines create a space in which the exploration of beliefs can occur in safety. In an interdenominational group that may include those who do not belong to a particular tradition or do not believe in a personal God, prayer, Bible study, and proselytizing would inhibit an open, nonjudgmental discussion. Over the years, when some members have asked that group members pray or read from the Bible, the leaders have reminded them that the focus of the group is on the discussion and understanding of beliefs, not on the exercises that might be associated with those beliefs.

Group Membership

Adult men and women, ranging in age from the late twenties to the sixties, have constituted the group over the years. One of the day treatment programs usually has ten to twelve group members; another has seven to ten. Diagnostically, group members have all suffered from a major mental illness: schizophrenia, delusional or bipolar disorder, major depression, schizoaffective disorder, or anxiety disorder. Religiously, they have been from different traditions: Jewish, Muslim, Catholic, Episcopalian, Methodist, Buddhist, and Baptist; some have been atheists and agnostics; some have been active in their tradition, others disaffected. Unlike the small sample reported in the Lindgren and Coursey study, the Jewish members of these groups have been active participants.

The group meets weekly for forty-five minutes and is co-led by the author (who is not a staff member at either treatment program) and an on-site staff member or intern. Initially we called the group the Religious Issues Group. When the members asserted that this narrowed the focus of the group unnecessarily, we changed the title to Spiritual Beliefs and Values Group.

Joining the group is voluntary but leaders ask for a commitment to ongoing attendance. Except for hospitalizations, absenteeism due to illness or weather, and the termination of treatment, the members have been highly consistent in attending the group.

Group Content and Process

When the group begins, each person is asked to describe his or her current religious affiliation or spiritual quest, as well as any changes in affiliation. New members, as they join, are asked the same questions, and current members share their histories again. This exchange serves to incorporate new members easily. The leaders share their religious tradition or spiritual path if they wish to do so. My own identity as a nun and psychologist is known in the community, whereas the staff person's religious tradition is not generally known. At times, some members of the group have had both positive and negative transference reactions but, generally, knowing the religious tradition of the leaders has not been problematic.

The groups are psychodynamically oriented rather than didactic. There is no set agenda. The leaders frequently ask what theme the group would like to focus on that day. If a long period of silence occurs at the beginning of the meeting, the leaders might explore the meaning of the silence. At times, the staff co-leader may relate the silence to some issues in the milieu—for example, a staff member leaving, a new intern coming, or another member attempting suicide.

Beliefs, values, and spiritual concerns are not accepted unquestioningly. The leaders relate what is said about beliefs to the person's life and current experience. A group member who seems to be using religion in a defensive way might be led to look at his or her beliefs as both aids and possible interferences in dealing with feelings and life in general. This is done by a guided exploration of how beliefs can help—or possibly what they may mean in the face of some tragedy. The client's willingness to consider the questions rather than react with anger, with a biblical quote, or with an accusation that the leaders are trying to undermine his or her faith helps the group to understand how the person is using his or her beliefs. The very existence of the group acknowledges that spirituality and religion are an important dimension in people's lives. Rather than viewing religion and spirituality as crutches that should be eliminated or outgrown, they are seen as areas to explore.

The group also struggles with the difficulties that are always present in groups of people with major mental illnesses: silence, hopelessness, dependence on leaders, difficulty in feeling a sense of the group, psychosis, resistance, and depression. In addition, the process over the years has revealed certain patterns, which have come to be predictable, with this population. Requests for more structure increase during holidays, during times of staff turnover, and after client suicides or attempted suicides.

There are similarities between the Spiritual Beliefs and Values group and other groups in the program. As in other treatment modalities, the therapeutic process focuses on family history, family messages, problematic relationships, emotions that are difficult to bear (anger, loneliness, hopelessness), suicidal ideation, questions about the meaning of life, and persons' senses of their experiences.

What light is shed on these clinical topics when they are discussed within the framework of the group? What are the unique features of the group? What is added to self-exploration when the lens of spiritual beliefs and values is used?

As an example of the group's process, consider this family message to a client struggling with anger and suicidality: "My mother said I was a bad person for wanting to do what I want to do, rather than what she wants me to do." When this message comes up in the group, the members discuss what makes a person bad, what evil is, how that is decided. They discuss whether there is a difference between what the individual wants, what the parents want, and what society wants. How does a person make a responsible decision about that? Is there a difference between being bad or evil and the bad feelings or urges that are a part of mental illness? Are people bad because of their mental illness? Are they to blame for their illness? Are families to blame? Group members often conclude that it is not their fault that they have a mental illness but then question how to deal with it. They pose many questions: If God is good, then why should they be afflicted with mental illness? If God is malevolent, then what hope do they have? Is mental illness a punishment from God? Because their individual beliefs differ, they learn that there are various ways of interpreting their shared experience of mental illness, thus breaking down a sense of isolation.

When anger is discussed, individuals question whether they can get angry at God, whether God is angry at them, whether their illness is a sign of God's abandoning them. When it is relevant to a person's religious tradition, the leaders may say, "In your tradition, are there examples of God's anger or are there examples of people crying out in anger toward God?" At times, the leaders may question whether maintaining a stance of anger toward God is a way of blaming God and avoiding responsibility for reality or possibly a way of avoiding other painful feelings such as sadness and loss.

The consideration of suicide raises the most basic questions about life, the meaning of life, the religious prohibitions about taking one's own life, and the factors that give people courage when they feel hopeless. When a member talked about her struggle with suicidal ideation, the others responded by sharing their own suicide attempts and their acceptance and concern for that member. The others made an effort to be a group memory for the member who seemed unable to access her own strength, meaning, hope, or beliefs. The group recognized that ultimately the client's life was her responsibility, but they evidenced a willingness to be with her while acknowledging their own fears and helplessness. The group has never focused on trying to persuade any person to stay alive nor have they tried to avoid the topic of suicide.

Other themes that the group discusses include questions about love: How can I love myself and my neighbor? If God is loving, why is there so much suffering? If there is no God, what is the meaning of it all? What is the difference between a spiritual experience and a psychotic experience? What gives life meaning and value? Why does each religion claim to have the truth?

Case Examples

The following material from two groups and a service that occurred at the time of a client's death illustrate the ways in which clients examine their beliefs, struggle with differences related to their beliefs, and use ritual to assist in the healing process. The names of the group members have been altered.

JIM: I have been reading Freud's *Future of An Illusion*. Freud says that science can't prove the existence of God and that human beings create the idea of God because they need God. That is precisely my dilemma. Science cannot prove the existence of God and faith cannot be verified by reason. Yet I know that I turn to religion for solace and comfort when I am feeling depressed and despondent.

ALICE: So that proves that Freud was right, that you create this need when you are feeling bad and it makes you feel better. I was never raised in any kind of religion, but sometimes I wish that I had something to turn to.

JIM: That is the strength and the weakness of the argument. Do human beings create the idea of God so that they will feel less hopeless and alone, or is there a God whose existence science can't prove and yet can't disprove, one who can be encountered in faith and that helps a person?

MARCIA: You all know that I always struggle with whether I believe or not, but I don't agree with the idea of creating God out of a need to feel less hopeless. On the contrary, it is when I am feeling better about myself, more in relation to other people, more caring, that I believe that there is some Goodness in the world that is greater than me, something that goes beyond me—a Force, a Spirit, a Higher Power. I'm not sure if it is a personal God.

SARAH: Some of you are much smarter than I am, but I believe in God and I know that God has helped me at times. I know I don't get it all, but I believe.

TOM: Science and faith don't have to be in contradiction to each other.

PETER: When I get more manicky, I get more religious and start thinking that I can save the world.

The discussion continued as illustrated. Individuals questioned each other, disagreed, shared their doubts, affirmed their beliefs, and left questions unresolved. More significantly, they could relate religion to, and separate it from, their illness.

The second case example occurred with a very different course at Passover. The groups in both settings regularly celebrate a Passover seder. Each year, in preparation for the seder, the leader explains the story of Passover. Because the groups are interdenominational, the leader explains the historical connection between the Passover seder and the Last Supper. Following one year's explanation, the following exchange occurred:

EVE: That makes me so angry. That means that Christians are appropriating a significant Jewish holiday. Once again, Christians are taking over. This has always been one of my favorite holidays.

RICHARD: Being Jewish in this culture means that who you are is devalued. This is a good example of how Jews feel oppressed.

JOHN: [Leader] is only showing us that there was a historical connection. Jesus was Jewish and so he was celebrating a seder.

CLAIRE: I am not going to participate in the seder. I don't like this discussion.

TOM: I believe in every word that the Bible says, and I have always believed that the Jews killed Jesus.

PETER: This is an example of why there are holy wars. Each religion wants to dominate the others and say it is the best.

EVE: Well, if we have a seder, I'm not coming.

TOM: I'm not, either.

LEADER: There have been many strong feelings expressed today and I think that it will be important for us to continue this discussion next week.

The tension and the differences of opinion in this meeting overflowed into the community and were the subject of community meetings, which involved clients who were not in the group. But the staff used this stimulus as an opportunity to talk about differences and tolerance. In group the following week, we continued to talk about the meaning of the seder as a memorial and a celebration that symbolizes the longings of all peoples to pass from slavery and oppression to freedom. We talked about how rooted people's beliefs are, how we can be shaped by the prejudices we have, and how difficult it is to talk about and to respect differences genuinely. One of the members challenged the leader when she said that she (as a Christian) was trying to take over a sacred Jewish holy day; others came to the leader's defense. It was the first time that the leader had been so challenged. By tolerating the strong expression of emotion, examining what individuals believe and how their beliefs make them feel oppressed and marginalized at times, and by continuing the discussion regardless, the group acknowledged they had done some difficult work and had understood how hard it is to respect differences. The group had weathered a crisis.

The ability of all participants in the program, both staff and clients, to work through this conflict was a sign of the commitment of the overall program to provide a safe place where individuals could talk about their feelings, and of the commitment of the Beliefs and Values Group to respect differences. The experience illustrates that the group members could question and confront both each other and the leader. They could listen, forgive, and claim their beliefs without devaluing others' beliefs. A host of anticipatory fears, expressed by the staff when the group first began, were thus not realized. No one in the program became more delusional. No one left the group or the program precipitously. No one's beliefs were shattered because of the discussion. In fact, members became aware of common ground with other beliefs and increased their levels of tolerance. Everyone in the program participated in the Passover seder that year.

The presence of the groups in a treatment milieu affords an additional opportunity: to have a memorial service at the time of a client's death. Over the course of the sixteen years that the groups have existed, clients in the day treatment programs, as well as on the inpatient unit, have died, due either to natural causes or suicides. (None of those who have committed suicide was a member of the Spiritual Beliefs and Values Group.) We have created a ritual memorial service that is nonsectarian so the community as a whole can acknowledge the loss and have an opportunity to express their thoughts and feelings about the deceased.

The following service was for Peter—a person with a long history in the mental health system, including difficulties in relationships with both care-givers and other members of the program, suicide attempts, and physical illness. Peter died unexpectedly of a heart attack; his death was a shock to all.

The memorial service began as usual with some classical music, followed by a reading drawn from the member's religious tradition. In this case that was appropriate; in other cases, we might use a suitable poem. Following the reading, time was provided for attendees to speak. In this particular service, those who had worked with Peter attested to his struggle to deal with his physical and psychic pain, his ongoing effort to assume responsibility for his life, and his involvement in a Christian community that gave him strength, hope, and a positive connectedness to a group of people who cared for him. Other members of the program recognized and named their anger, their frustrating experiences with him when he would reject them, their guilt at not being more responsive—and yet their knowledge of how he had grown over the years. The community expressed their sense of Peter with truth, compassion, and emotion. Psychological understanding did not negate religious belief, and religious belief was not used to deny pain.

In the sixteen-year history of the group, members have acknowledged that the groups have often posed a challenge to their beliefs. Members have questioned their beliefs and re-thought previously learned religious messages. At different times, two individuals have left the group because they were threatened by the discussion and said they were leaving because they "wanted to preserve their faith." Occasionally, individuals have come to the group in the grips of a delusion. But no one over the sixteen years has become *more* delusional because of the group. On the contrary, members have discussed intelligently the differences between a delusion and a religious experience. Some recognize that when they are becoming more religious, they are cycling into a manic episode. Others recognize that when they are improving, they become more interested in religion, as noted in the example given earlier.

Six years ago, when one of the groups celebrated its tenth anniversary, we talked about the meaning of the group for the members. They said, "This is the most challenging group in the program. It isn't always easy to look at what you believe; in this group, I learned that it was OK to be angry at God and at some of the things the church has done to me. I was pestered to death by my grand-mother about religion, but here I learned that I have a spiritual quest that can be separated from religion. This group got me interested in the spiritual issues of the mentally ill. I have learned a lot about other religions and it seems to me that we have a lot in common. There ought to be a U.N. for religions so peo-ple can sit around and talk like we do and learn from each other." A staff per-son said, "This is one of the most important groups in the program. It respects the strengths of the clients and focuses on their abilities rather than their dis-abilities."

Conclusion

Sixteen years of experience refute the often-stated view that the introduction of religious issues into treatment will encourage a client's delusional thoughts and destructively reinforce defenses. At times the group has been able to deal with a member who was delusional at that moment and enable him or her to calm down in the group. At other times, we have had to ask a person to leave the group and come back the following week because the person's delusions were disrupting the group. The presence of a full-time staff member has inte-grated the group into the treatment context and militated against splitting. Rather than using the group to avoid therapeutic work or to avoid pain or escape into a fantasy world of religious beliefs, the members have consistently tried to relate what they believe to their life situation. The value of such relat-ing is recognized by the staff. But for the members, one of the most significant aspects of the group is the exposure to the beliefs of others and the recogni-tion that, despite differences in dogmatic aspects of belief, all men and women search for answers to similar questions and even have similar answers to fun-damental questions, though they may use different language.

Therapy provides clients with a safe place, yet many clients do not feel that individual therapy or group therapy is a safe enough place to talk about their religious or spiritual beliefs. The Spiritual Beliefs and Values Group cre-ates a forum in which the questions that clients have about the meaning of life, the meaning of suffering, and God's role in suffering, can be discussed without the fear of being labeled dismissively as psychotic. The groups enable individ-uals to reflect on what they believe, to explore their beliefs, to be questioned, to listen to the diverse ways in which others make sense of their suffering, to distinguish between their illness and spiritual experiences. In the group, the members seek to explore their beliefs as they fit the particulars of their own mental life.

Religious-issues groups, therefore, meet unaddressed needs of the seri-ously mentally ill, offering an opportunity to explore issues usually slighted by mainstream mental health practice. Properly guided in nonjudgmental and nonproselytizing directions, such groups provide valuable therapeutic experi-ences in the realms of tolerance, acceptance of others' views, thoughtful examination of belief systems, and opportunities to apply spirituality and values to life questions.

References

Byrd, R. B. "Positive Therapeutic Effects of Intercessory Prayer in a Coronary Care Unit Population." *Southern Medical Journal,* 1988, *81,* 826–829.

Gartner, J., Larson, D. B., and Allen, G. D. "Religious Commitment and Mental Health: A Review of the Empirical Literature." *Journal of Psychology and Theology,* 1991, *19,* 6–25.

Genia, V. "Interreligious Encounter Group: A Psychospiritual Experience for Faith Development." *Counseling and Values,* 1990, *35* (1), 39–51.

Koenig, H. G. *Is Religion Good for Your Health? Effects of Religion on Mental and Physical Health.* New York: Haworth Press, 1997.

Kroll, J., and Sheehan, W. "Religious Beliefs and Practices among 52 Psychiatric Inpatients in Minnesota." *American Journal of Psychiatry,* 1989, *146,* 67–72.

Levin, J. S. "Religious Factor in Aging, Adjustment, and Health: A Theoretical Overview." In W. M. Clements (ed.), *Religion, Aging and Health: A Global Perspective.* New York: Haworth Press, 1989.

Lindgren, K., and Coursey, R. "Spirituality and Serious Mental Illness: A Two-Part Study." *Psychiatric Rehabilitation Journal,* 1995, *18* (3), 93–111.

Matthews, D. A., Larson, D. B., and Barry, C. P. *The Faith Factor: An Annotated Bibliography of Clinical Research on Spiritual Subjects,* Vol. 3: *Enhancing Life Satisfaction.* Rockville, Md.: National Institute for Healthcare Research, 1993.

O'Rourke, C. "Exploring Spiritual Issues of Adults with Mental Illness in Group Psychotherapy." *Smith College Studies in Social Work,* 1997, *67* (2),177–196.

Pargament, K., Olsen, H., Reilly, B., Falgouot, K., Ensing, D. S., and Van Haitsma, K. "God Help Me: The Relationship of Religious Orientations to Religious Coping with Negative Life Events." *Journal for the Scientific Study of Religion,* 1992, *31,* 504–513.

Sullivan, W. P. "It Helps Me to Be a Whole Person: The Role of Spirituality among the Mentally Challenged." *Psychosocial Rehabilitation Journal,* 1993, *16* (3), 125–134.

Worthington, E. L., Kurusu, T. A., and McCullough, M. E. "Empirical Research on Religion and Psychotherapeutic Processes and Outcomes: A 10-Year Review and Research Prospectus." *Psychological Bulletin,* 1996, *119* (3), 448–487.

NANCY C. KEHOE is instructor in psychology at the Cambridge Health Alliance, which is affiliated with Harvard Medical School; she is a member of the Religious of the Sacred Heart.

In a mind-body group designed to address issues of well-being for people with severe mental disorders, experiences with spiritual themes of optimal functioning and ultimate meaning emerged with surprising clarity.

Spiritual Dimensions of a Mind-Body Group for People with Severe Mental Illness

David W. Freeman, Rebecca Wolfson, H.-Urs Affolter

Community-based treatment for people with severe mental illness has become increasingly holistic. Emphasis is not only on psychiatric and residential stability but on helping people develop potential in many life domains, including physical and emotional well-being, recreation, education, work, social and intimate relationships, and spirituality. Mind-body techniques and groups, which certainly fit with key goals of consumer recovery, well-being, and empowerment, are underutilized parts of this more holistic orientation. Because of widespread heart-related physical and medical problems among our clients and high levels of poorly managed stress, Community Connections—a comprehensive, urban mental health agency serving many people with severe mental disorders—developed a Healthy Heart Group that uses mind-body techniques to promote physical and emotional well-being and consumer self-care. Although these goals were at the center of the group's activities, we did not anticipate the extent to which spiritual concerns would emerge in the group.

The purpose of this chapter is to discuss the spiritual dimensions of the Healthy Heart Group. We understand spirituality as a broad dimension of human experience. It may involve, for example, experiences of optimal or peak functioning (Maslow, 1954), "flow" experiences (Csikszentmihalyi, 1990), mystical and near-death encounters (Lukoff, Lu, and Turner, 1992), or movements toward intimacy and mutuality in relationships (Clinebell, 1984).

To put the Healthy Heart Group in context, we describe some mind-body techniques, as well as the hopes and concerns we have about applying those techniques in work with people who have severe mental illnesses. We recommend adaptations of the techniques for this population and describe the agency context of the intervention and of group membership, structure, and content. We then discuss the spiritual issues that emerged in the course of the clinical intervention.

Mind-Body Interventions

Interest in the interaction between mind and body in healing processes has fueled an enormous growth of interest in alternative medicine and health psychology during the past decade. Advances in psychoneuroimmunology (Ader, Cohen, and Felten, 1995), for example, have helped establish the mind-body interaction within the purview of scientific study, and documentation of the success of mind-body techniques is rapidly expanding. Benson (1975), Ornish (1990), and Borysenko (1987) are among the many research-practitioners who have identified in their research the beneficial effects of these practices. An additional legitimacy has been added to mind-body techniques through the Office of Alternative Medicine at the National Institutes of Health.

Although some mind-body techniques have been practiced for millennia (for example, yoga and meditation), only recently have they gained widespread popularity in this culture. In fact, *alternative medicine* may now be a misnomer, as consumers spend billions of dollars on these techniques, and the best-seller lists are often filled with guides to new popularizations of mind-body techniques (for example, Weil, 1995). Indeed, many aspects of alternative medicine have been incorporated in mainstream medical practice (including yoga, biofeedback, acupuncture, chiropractic, therapeutic massage, guided meditation, autogenic phrases, breathing practices, and progressive muscle relaxation). Even less-well-known alternative interventions (Qi Gong, therapeutic touch, somatoemotional release, and polarity therapy) are being evaluated by traditional health insurance carriers as potentially reimbursable services.

Hopes and Concerns About Using Mind-Body Techniques for People with Severe Mental Disorders

There are many reasons to be hopeful about using mind-body techniques with people diagnosed with severe mental disorders. Mind-body techniques are often practiced in empowerment and well-being models of treatment, which makes them particularly attractive to many consumer advocates of care for people with severe mental illness (Dincin, 1995). Mind-body techniques, furthermore, are designed to facilitate stress management, improve self-control, and enhance quality of life. These techniques help people optimize experiences of enjoyment and pleasure (Csikszentmihalyi, 1990). They create opportunities for people to cultivate the peak experiences that give a depth of meaning to life (Maslow, 1954) and are supportive of connectedness and mutuality in relationships (Clinebell, 1984). Clinical strategies that support optimal functioning will address gaps in a service delivery system that has traditionally emphasized stabilization through external management and control of symptoms and behavior.

Clinicians also have reason to be concerned about the application of mind-body techniques with people who have severe mental disorders. Clinicians working with these individuals can be focused on helping the consumer meet basic needs: proper medical and psychiatric care, financial benefits, housing, treatment for co-occurring disorders such as addictions, and help with family crises. Other aspects of the person's quality of life may not get the proper attention when clinicians are so occupied. The practical factors of time, energy, and money may serve as barriers to the development and use of new interventions with this population.

Clinicians may also be concerned that the symptoms associated with severe mental illnesses will undermine the effectiveness of mind-body techniques. Concrete thinking and disruptions of attention, for example, might impair the imaginative use of metaphor and imagery. (In fact, we did encounter incidents of group members' concrete thinking during discussions of safe places. One client who was thinking of physical safety became focused on the police response to noise in her apartment building. Even this client, however, was able to shift from the concrete to the more abstract and joined in a discussion about emotional safety as well.) Some clinicians may fear that psychotic symptoms will worsen during a relaxed trance. Others have suggested that dissociative processes, which are therapeutically facilitated in mind-body work, may become destructive if the client's trauma history and the impact of trauma-related symptoms on the dissociative process are not well understood. In all these cases, the clinician may fear that the patient could lose control, decompensate, and be unable to regain internal equilibrium.

Applying Mind-Body Techniques for People with Severe Mental Disorders

In the absence of a substantial literature on the use of mind-body interventions with this population, we developed a highly structured six-week group that systematically exposed clients to a series of mind-body techniques.

Having three group leaders allowed for a comfortable distribution of complex clinical tasks. For example, clinicians could rotate among the various roles of managing the overall pace of the session, leading the group in an experiential exercise, and focusing on how the individual members were handling the material. Three leaders also gave us the flexibility to attend to individual crises should they occur (although we did not have problems with crises in this group). Leaders met before and after each group to discuss how each group member responded, to identify trouble spots, to share opinions about what worked, and to plan adjustments in future sessions. Because of the agency setting, we often saw our clients in the office for other appointments and were able to maintain informal contact between weekly group sessions. We checked in with the clients to see how they were doing, encouraged them to come to the next group session, expressed how much we were enjoying their participation in the group, and offered the opportunity for them to speak individually with us about any difficulties, questions, or concerns.

All three leaders had been working with adults with severe mental illness and studying mind-body interventions for several years. We felt confident in our ability to notice signs of decompensation and to be able to differentiate between psychotic and nonpsychotic processes. The literature suggests that the integration of a new, profound, and searching clinical technique should only be used when the clinician is otherwise familiar with the population (Hodge, 1990).

We modified group inductions to allow individuals to create their own zone of safety within the group. For example, clients were encouraged to keep their eyes open during guided meditations if they felt safer that way. We allowed time for checking in at the beginning of each group and ample time for discussion of the meditative experience in each group.

The Healthy Heart Group at Community Connections

We tailored the group's content and structure to meet the particular needs of consumers at Community Connections.

Agency Context. Most consumers at Community Connections share experiences of social victimization, substance abuse, severe and persistent mental illness, and a history of homelessness. Mind-body services are, therefore, provided in the context of a full-service agency that provides intensive clinical case management, trauma recovery, substance abuse, housing, and psychiatric services. The Healthy Heart Group is open to any member of Community Connections who has a history of physical problems, including high blood pressure, angina, and other heart and circulatory difficulties, as well as psychological difficulties in relation to self and other.

Group Goals. The Healthy Heart Group is designed to be supportive of participant motivation, engagement, well-being, and self-care. The secondary purpose of the group is to explore the usefulness and impact of mind-body techniques with people who have severe mental disorders.

Although it is premature to generalize from this group's experience to the wider population of individuals with severe mental illness, it is striking that none of the women experienced psychotic decompensation, destructive dissociative processes, or unmanageable anxiety in this group. In fact, they expressed a strong sense of connection to each other and to the leaders, and managed their own sense of safety in the room. In a very short time they developed a strong sense of group identification and wanted a parting ritual at the end of the group to say a proper goodbye.

Group Membership. All participants had histories of heart disease, high blood pressure, and other medical problems, in addition to having trouble managing stress. Four members were consistent participants in the group—all

African American women. Their symptoms varied, but all of the women struggled intermittently with severe psychotic, dissociative, and affective difficulties. Several group members had a co-occurring substance abuse disorder. All had extensive histories of homelessness and hospitalization.

Group Structure. We interviewed each prospective group member individually and evaluated medical history, current symptoms, and current problems. We explained what we meant by the mind-body connection and did a brief breathing exercise with them to demonstrate that technique. We asked what they would like to get out of the group experience and let them know that we wanted to help them increase their own capacity to cope with stressful situations and increase their sense of personal power.

The Healthy Heart Group used several mind-body techniques, including progressive muscle relaxation, guided meditation, biofeedback, exercise and stretching, autogenic phrases, and breathing exercises. We used "safe place" imagery, "inner guide" imagery, and imagery about forgiveness. We did not use age regression techniques and confusion techniques, as we judged those to be the most potentially destabilizing techniques with this population.

At the beginning of each session we reviewed any questions or concerns left over from the week before. We found that clients practiced each week by repeating an autogenic phrase or using a bit of imagery to help them relax. We had a psychoeducationally structured discussion of a different topic each week, including stress and the autonomic nervous system, breathing, safety, the use of inner guides in thinking about the past and the future, relaxation and the use of autogenic phrases, and forgiveness. The session that included exercises on safe places and inner guides launched discussions of death, pain, loss, love, grief, and health.

Spirituality in the Healthy Heart Group

The goal of the Healthy Heart Group was to do mind-body work, but participants spontaneously brought up issues that point to spiritual dimensions of experience. In our understanding, spirituality is expressed in mind-body work through experiences that are intense, full, deeply satisfying, and reflective of optimal well-being. Many authors have described these spiritually oriented experiences. Lukoff, Lu, and Turner (1992) suggest that nonpathological, psychospiritual issues are often organized around near-death and mystical experiences. Mind-body practices may also facilitate a person's ability to enter into individual and collective states of competent efficiency that Csikszentmihalyi (1990) describes so lucidly as "flow," that is, a state of optimal experience that is fully absorbing and genuinely satisfying. Clients also reported having experiences in group that are akin to Maslow's (1954) widely recognized peak experiences. Most of these discussions were characterized by a courageous spontaneity, a vivid intensity, a creative vitality, and an unusual degree of honesty with self and others. Healthy Heart members used the group experience to discuss fundamental spiritual and existential concerns with loss, grief, and death, as well as safety, trust, responsibility, joy, and love. In addition to these individually oriented experiences, the social connections that developed in the course of this short-term group and the discussed experiences of closeness and care highlighted a relational dimension of spirituality. Here, optimal experience is seen in an enhanced sense of belonging and mutuality in relationships.

The success of the discussions of fundamental life concerns like love and death with such a marginalized population is exceptional. Consumers at Community Connections can be apathetic, withdrawn, dissociated, or disorganized, and correspondingly unsuccessful in sharing experiences with other people. This group provided both the structure and the technique to bring out the best of each client's social skills. Instead of withdrawal and hopeless despair, there was a sense of concern and urgency in this group. Instead of disorganization, there was a sense of purpose and meaning. Instead of withdrawal, there was an active social involvement with group members and group leaders. Instead of confusion, there was a sense of clarity and hopefulness.

Optimal Functioning with the Support of Mind-Body Practice

The Healthy Heart Group helped members optimize personal functioning in a variety of ways: heightened self-awareness, increased openness and genuine expression, greater vitality, and more energy. Names and other identifying information have been altered to protect participants' privacy. The experiences of Christine Edwards—a forty-five-year-old, widowed, African American woman diagnosed with schizoaffective disorder and high blood pressure—reflect many of these attributes. Prior to the full development of her mental illness, she had a successful marriage and a relatively stable work history. Since her first psychotic episode, she has had at least twenty years of mental health treatment in a variety of forms, including hospitalization, psychotherapy, day treatment, and case management. She has generally been regarded as an exceptionally difficult client with a borderline personality disorder in addition to her Axis I diagnosis. Her psychiatric decompensations typically require at least six months of hospitalization before she can regain her baseline level of function.

In the last session of the group, Edwards wondered aloud why group members had been so "open, honest, and bold" in the course of the group experience. This characterization of the group highlighted the members' genuineness, spontaneity, and clarity—key features of optimal functioning. In the ensuing discussion, group members came to the consensus that the relaxation and imagery used in weekly meditations and inductions, together with discussion of the meditative experiences in group, helped members mobilize and consolidate their most productive energies. Members, for example, were able to spontaneously discuss intense personal experiences and long-held secrets (including, for example, having loving feelings for others and attempting suicide). Indeed, much of the discussion in the group had a strong, energetic, and absorbing quality that is often not evident in other kinds of groups with similar membership. Edwards also seemed accurate in her description of the surprising directness in the group. After the meditative experiences, group members were able to give group leaders very direct and honest feedback about personal and professional strengths and limitations. Edwards, for example, spoke of her love for one of the group leaders and her feeling that another group leader was still too new to the clinical process. She was able to describe these compliments and criticisms in a nondefensive, direct, and compassionate manner.

Edwards feels a deep sense of discomfort and grief related to her mental illness, her loss of the capacity to work consistently, and the multiple losses of family members. In the course of the group, she identified her sense of shame, in particular, as an issue that had caused her significant problems in coping with difficult life experiences. At first she was uncomfortable with, and rejecting of, the experience of shame, but as the group continued, she identified the feeling as one she hopes to better understand in the future. This realization came to her most clearly in the "soft belly" exercise—a guided meditation in softening and opening the body so as to allow for greater sensitivity to internal psychological and physical states and experiences. Initially, she was very concrete and focused on her negative feelings about being overweight. After some discussion, however, she demonstrated a clearer understanding of the unique blend of the metaphorical and the concrete in mind-body work, observing, "I hide in my soft belly." She then wanted to identify and understand the feelings and memories she had "tucked away." In this manner, Edwards used the group to increase her motivation for self-awareness, self-understanding, and self-acceptance.

Edwards also used the group to strengthen her sense of self as a buffer against recurring psychiatric symptoms. She had a regular history of entering the hospital for long-term stays during the Christmas holidays and the anniversary of her husband's death. The Healthy Heart Group ended just before the Christmas holiday, and for the first time in twenty years she was able to stay out of the hospital. She attributed her capacity to maintain her psychiatric stability to the relaxation and imagery skills she had learned in the group.

Near-Death Experiences. Many individuals find spiritual meaning in facing the boundaries of life and death that emerge in near-death experiences (Lukoff, Lu, and Turner, 1992). Donna Barnes brought the group's attention to the ultimate connections between life and death in the third group session. Barnes is a sixty-year-old, single, African American woman who is a mother and grandmother. She has a long history of auditory hallucinations that are often resistant to medication, as well as substantial problems with angina and periodic fears that she is having a heart attack. In previous psychotherapy group experiences with these co-leaders, Barnes had a tendency to withdraw, talk to herself, or engage with others in a friendly but superficial manner. In the Healthy Heart Group, Barnes allowed herself to enter deep trance states with relative ease. She had an exceptionally trusting attitude toward the meditative process. Group members first settled into a relaxed discussion of their practice experiences with the autogenic phrases exercise (in which each individual used repeated, self-soothing phrases, usually focused on bodily sensations, to deepen relaxation and minimize anxiety). Barnes then described how an old friend with whom she had once meditated regularly used the image of entering a bright white light to facilitate the deepening of the trance state. When another group member remarked that people sometimes see a bright white light just before dying, the group entered into a lively discussion of near-death experiences. Barnes then explained that she had come close to death during a suicide attempt by gassing—an incident that she had not discussed in the previous seven years of group treatment. Barnes brought a dignified intensity to the story of her suicide attempt. Her ability to initiate and then participate in the discussion with such grace, focus, and organization seemed to reflect the strength that she had drawn from the mind-body exercises.

Barnes's description of her suicide attempt brought the subject of death into the shared group experience in a way that was profoundly moving for group members and co-leaders. The emotional power and intimate immediacy and vulnerability of Barnes's story evoked in leaders and other group members feelings about their own mortality and prompted all of us to reflect on our own reasons for living. This session put us all in mind of ultimate questions of meaning in the context of life and death issues. Barnes was caring for her infant son at the time of the suicide attempt and, although she had opened a window in his room so he would not suffocate in the gassing, she had not previously realized that he had been in serious danger. Neither had she grappled with her feelings about hurting or abandoning her son. The group was confronted, therefore, with both suicidal and homicidal issues. As the group witnessed the threat to life, each member attempted to reassert the fundamental value of life in her or his own way. Clinicians, for example, had to resist the tendency to withdraw into an overly analytical and defended position. After hearing Barnes's story, another group member broke out into a full-throated gospel hymn. At first, group members and leaders regarded her song as bizarre, but we eventually came to understand her singing as a mechanism for restoring a sense of order and peace.

Belonging and Mutuality in Relationships. All of the authors who describe human efforts to achieve optimal functioning describe the central importance of mutuality in relationships. Clinebell (1984) notes that one of the effects of growth-facilitating spirituality is precisely this sense of mutual connection and commitment to other persons. In our group, Lucinda Ward was able to use the ambience created by mind-body practice to enter into new and unexpected relationships. Ward is a fifty-year-old woman who has been diagnosed with a severe mental illness most of her adult life. She came to Community Connections after having been evicted from her family home by her daughter who, despite a severe drug addiction, had assumed control of the home and the lease. At the agency, Ward is very reclusive and avoids involvement with others. She was referred to the Healthy Heart Group because of problems with high blood pressure and because her clinician had a rather vague hope that she would be able to make productive use of the psychosocial support.

Ward stayed to herself in the group until we had a discussion about responsibility and care for others. This discussion developed in the context of a meditative exercise using safe place imagery. In this technique, group members describe places they consider safe, then construct a narrative around the safe place, and finally visit the place in their imagination. As members described their images of a safe place, there were frequent references to grandmothers' homes, the comfort of relationships with pets, and religious sanctuary. Discussion of safe place imagery prompted several group members to describe their experiences in caring for sick and elderly loved ones. Group members were then able to freely discuss the guilt, shame, and burden they felt in assuming the caretaker responsibility, especially when they were themselves so disabled by mental and physical illnesses. Ward emerged from the background in this group discussion and shared her story of her mother's experiences in a nursing home. During weekly visits, Ward regularly requested special attention from hospital staff to keep her mother from getting out of bed without proper support. She was regularly ignored. On several occasions, Ward's mother had fallen as a result of the inadequate supervision and support, and Ward was afraid her mother would suffer a more severe injury. Eventually, Ward's fears came true: her mother suffered a more serious fall and then died as a complication of the head injury she had sustained. Ward was able to tell the story with a full range of feeling, with expressiveness that seemed totally out of character for her. Ward's story about her mother was echoed by other group members who had also struggled with the issues of caring for disabled parents. Joyce Smith's mother, for example, spent much of her adult life in an institution for people with both developmental disability and mental illness, and Smith shared her feelings about not being able to care for her mother in a more independent setting. The group had become a safe place itself, creating a safe enough environment for members to comfortably share their most heart-felt stories.

Mystical Experiences. Mystical experiences provide us with a connection to the transcendent dimensions of life and can facilitate the inner enrichment and growth that comes with this type of peak experience. Mystical experiences help sustain the basic wonder and mystery of all life and encourage heightened aliveness, joy, and celebration of life (Clinebell, 1984; Maslow, 1954).

This dimension of spirituality emerged most clearly in clients' development of safe place imagery. Clients identified religious sanctuary, heaven, nature, and old family homes as images that could be the focus of safe place imagery. In all the guided meditations, we emphasized each member's opportunity for control of the mind-body experience. For example, we gave permission for people to leave their eyes open or closed during meditations, whichever felt more comfortable. We emphasized the normal human need for self-protection and the variety of defenses we employ to manage our feelings. We explained that the techniques used in our group could be additional strategies to cope with stressors and that group members were in control of their experience with the experiential exercises and could use them to the extent they felt safe and comfortable. Participants were able to use these images to cultivate a sense of calm, peace, and safety.

Joyce Smith, for example, used the group to develop relaxation techniques that were, by turn, both self-soothing and quietly ecstatic. Smith is a thirty-five-year-old African American woman with a diagnosis of schizophrenia and high blood pressure. She has an extensive history of severe anxiety in response to stressors in her relationship with her mother. She was able to derive great pleasure and satisfaction from the safe place imagery she learned in the group, as she calmed and soothed herself after difficult episodes of anxiety. As a general rule, Smith appears confused and disoriented, but she told these success stories with an air of gentle calm and wonder.

Several group members described childhood memories of time spent in the country or on a farm, visiting a grandfather's home in the country, or walking in a clearing in the woods. When cultivating safe place images, Christine Edwards described a memory of watching a squirrel leap from branch to branch, as if it were savoring the joy of being alive. In her description she captured the mystical qualities of a universalizing experience of oneness with nature. The value we attributed to this memory supported Edwards's enjoyment of spontaneity and beauty in nature. As she described the image, it was as if she was telling us that for her, beauty gives meaning to life.

Conclusion

The Healthy Heart Group at Community Connections is a clinical intervention that uses mind-body techniques to address physical and emotional problems of the heart. Spiritual resources can make a contribution to helping with these problems of the heart. Mind-body techniques are, by definition, holistic in nature and are facilitative of growth-enhancing spiritual experiences. We anticipated discussion of somatic complaints, emotional difficulties, and some spiritual concerns. Although members certainly reported changes in some physical and emotional self-care activities, we did not anticipate the extent to which spiritual concerns would be addressed in the group. As a way of thinking about some of the clinical and spiritual issues that emerged in this mind-body group, this chapter reports several examples of experiences related to optimal human functioning, to near-death experiences, and to mutuality in relationships.

References

Ader, R., Cohen, N., and Felten, D. "Psychoneuroimmunology: Interactions Between the Nervous System and the Immune System." *Lancet*, 1995, *345,* 99–103.

Benson, H. *The Relaxation Response.* New York: Avon Books, 1975.

Borysenko, J. *Minding the Body, Mending the Mind.* New York: Bantam Books, 1987.

Clinebell, H. *Basic Types of Pastoral Care and Counseling.* Nashville: Abingdon Press, 1984.

Csikszentmihalyi, M. *Flow: The Psychology of Optimal Experience.* New York: Harper Perennial, 1990.

Dincin, J. (ed.). *A Pragmatic Approach to Psychiatric Rehabilitation: Lessons from Chicago's Thresholds Program.* New Directions for Mental Health Services, no. 68. San Francisco: Jossey-Bass, 1995.

Hodge, J. R. "Can Hypnosis Help Psychosis?" In D. C. Hammond (ed.), *Handbook of Hypnotic Suggestions and Metaphors.* New York: Norton, 1990.

Lukoff, D., Lu, F., and Turner, R. "Toward a More Culturally Sensitive DSM-IV: Psychoreligious and Psychospiritual Problems." *Journal of Nervous and Mental Disease,* 1992, *180* (11), 673–682.

Maslow, A. *Motivation and Personality.* New York: Harper, 1954.

Maslow, A. *Toward a Psychology of Being.* New York: Van Nostrand Reinhold, 1968.

Ornish, D. *Reversing Heart Disease.* New York: Ivy Books, 1990.

Weil, A. *Spontaneous Healing.* New York: Fawcett Columbine, 1995.

DAVID W. FREEMAN *is clinical supervisor at Community Connections in Washington, D.C., and is in private practice in Chevy Chase, Maryland.*

REBECCA WOLFSON *is administrative director and clinical social worker at the Community Connections Mental Health Center.*

H.-URS AFFOLTER *is clinical case manager at Community Connections, a certified clinical hypnotherapist, and a facilitator and instructor at the Center for Mind-Body Medicine in Washington, D.C.*

Innovative programs developed by faith communities for people with mental illness, as well as guidelines for collaboration between religious and mental health organizations, are presented.

The Faith Community as a Support for People with Mental Illness

Jennifer Shifrin

The Reverend Craig Rennebohm has found in his work as a mental health chaplain that "the church can be a primary base for organizing the community to do ministries that change society, transform individual lives and create a community of compassion" (Stamp, 1993, p. 1). For people with mental illness the church and synagogue are credible, stable organizations that can give long-term, ongoing support and opportunities for integration. These communities have a long history of developing organized responses to the concerns that affect their members and those they serve, including individuals with mental illness. Such responses provide opportunities to integrate people with mental illness into the life of the congregation and the community and to develop educational and service projects.

Examples of Faith Community Programs

The programs of several congregations illustrate some of the ways in which faith communities have responded to the needs of people with mental illness.

Pilgrim Congregational United Church of Christ (UCC). When Craig Rennebohm was pastor of the Pilgrim Congregational UCC, he came to the realization that about one-third of the people who came to the church shelter program also had a mental illness. In response to their needs, he established the Mental Health Chaplaincy program in 1987, with the support of the Church Council of Greater Seattle. The program trains lay people from area congregations to be companions to people who are formerly homeless and who have mental illness. It also brings together representatives of area congregations and mental health programs to raise awareness about mental illness and to advocate for public policy reform. In addition to supporting the chaplaincy program, Pilgrim offers a support group for people to pray and share concerns and resources for people with mental illness.

As Pilgrim's program became better known in the Seattle area, other congregations began to develop similar services. Plymouth Congregational UCC, for example, has trained its membership to be welcoming and to listen to people in distress who attend Sunday services. This congregation also provides crisis beds in its low-income apartments. Prospect UCC offers a midweek vesper service for people who are homeless or have mental illness (Stamp, 1993). University Presbyterian Church founded a Mental Health Ministry program that includes outreach and support services, support groups for consumers and families, a spiritual support group for mental health workers, recreational programs, and a Bible study and fellowship group for consumers and families.

First United Methodist Church. The First United Methodist Church in Tulsa, Oklahoma, is a five-thousand-member congregation of long standing in the downtown area. After mental illness was brought to this congregation's attention, the church responded with a program called the Second MILERS (MILE stands for Mental Illness a Loving Embrace). It is a multifaceted program to serve people with mental illness, their families, and the mental health community. Since 1993, the congregation, in partnership with the Mental Health Association of Tulsa, has hosted interfaith prayer services focused on mental illness during Mental Illness Awareness Week. The church has educated five hundred families through the Journey of Hope program, which is presented by trained volunteers from the congregation. For the past five years, the local Consumer Council has held its annual conferences at the church. In 1995, Second MILE Outreach began a partnership with Mobile Crisis Services to form Critical Transition Care Teams to befriend formerly homeless people with mental illness as they made the transition to residential stability. When the congregation learned that funding for the Mobile Crisis Services was not included in the appropriations bill for the coming year, the congregation wrote to the Oklahoma Senate, circulated petitions in support of the program, and organized a prayer effort to support inclusion of funding for this program. The funding was restored and the program is continuing.

North Presbyterian Church. In the 1970s, people with mental illness living in the community surrounding North Presbyterian Church in Kalamazoo, Michigan, began attending services and eventually joining this small congregation of fewer than one hundred members. Today, half the congregation are mental health consumers. In 1977, the congregation formed a Mental Health Mission Group. It grew into the Community Mission Group that initiated the first soup kitchen in Kalamazoo and a drop-in and referral center. By 1989 the congregation realized that people with mental illness are often unable to participate in many activities because of financial limitations, fear, and anxiety. A committee addressed this concern by forming The Togetherness Group, which was composed of church members and mental health consumers in the community. The members meet once a month and not only participate in a number of social activities (having picnics; going to movies, plays, and concerts; and bowling) but also visit people at a regional psychiatric facility and at nursing homes. The congregation, with only eleven full-time employed members, has limited resources and receives annual assistance from the Presbyterian Church (U.S.A.) of $4,000 to support these activities (Kraft, 1991; Cunningham, 1997).

Shared Values in the Faith and Mental Health Communities

How can the mental health community encourage other caring responses to mental illness in congregations that have no overt exposure to mental illness? The first step is to understand that the faith and mental health communities share values that provide a philosophical basis for developing a working relationship. The faith and mental health communities see themselves as agents of care and healing. Both communities share the goal of being compassionate toward those they serve and creating an atmosphere of acceptance. Both believe people are social beings who need one another, not only for companionship but also for finding meaning in life. Both agree that people have an enhanced prognosis when they are able to participate in supportive community settings. Both encourage and support people in making or renewing friendships and in developing or recovering social networks as well as vocational and recreational skills. Both work with people to help them overcome feelings of despair and powerlessness. Both focus on promoting self-esteem and nurturing the human spirit. Both encourage people to live with what is possible in the present but also to recognize the hope the future holds (Anderson, 1990).

The Faith Community

The faith community of churches and synagogues in the United States comprises at least 100 denominations, 300,000 congregations, and 120 million people. A majority of these congregations have between 100 and 399 members; about one-third have over 400 members, and the remainder have 100 members or fewer (Hodgkinson and others, 1993).

Faith Group Resources. Surveys by the INDEPENDENT SECTOR found approximately 75 percent of those who responded reported that they had attended church in the past year and that 70 percent were members of a church or synagogue. About 52 percent gave cash contributions to the congregation, and 58 percent volunteered either within their congregation or the larger community (Hodgkinson and others, 1993).

Ninety percent of the congregations reported programs in human services, health, and welfare; 90 percent reported one or more health programs; and 87 percent reported involvement in programs of visitation or support for sick people and for shut-ins. Forty-seven percent stated that they not only had programs within their congregations but also in affiliation with other agencies. Ninety percent reported that their facilities were used by groups within the congregations, and 60 percent said that their facilities were used by outside community groups (Hodgkinson and others, 1993).

These statistics demonstrate that congregations can be a powerful resource for the mental health community. In order for mental health professionals and organizations to work more effectively with the faith community, a clear conception of the congregation's self-understanding, its structure, and history is essential.

Faith Group Structure. The congregation itself is a natural, organic community. Each congregation consists of people who come together for worship, fellowship, and service to members of their congregation and the larger community. Other voluntary associations such as the Optimists or Rotary, or special interest groups such as the National Alliance for the Mentally Ill or the American Cancer Society, are brought together by a common cause, but they do not have the bond of a common set of religious beliefs, values, and history that are inherent in congregations and faith groups.

A congregation is an entity within a larger structure—the faith group. The faith group is an organization, some would say a bureaucracy, with a structure and entry points to offices and committees whose task is to respond to the needs of various constituencies. In most denominations, organized responses to the needs of people who are physically impaired or developmentally disabled have existed for years. In the past few years, many denominations have turned their attention to mental illness. Each faith group has routes through its structure at the congregational, local, regional, and national levels. These routes can lead to action by the denomination in responding to mental illness. For some denominations, mental illness is a health issue, for some a disabilities issue, for some a social justice issue, for some an education issue, and for some a combination of all four.

It is important when working with a local congregation or faith group office to learn the history of the response of its denomination to mental illness. Sixteen major denominations in the Jewish and Christian traditions have a policy statement on mental illness. When a position is taken on an issue like mental illness, a call to action is generally part of the group's policy. This call gives legitimacy to turning the congregation's attention to mental illness. It lays out the theological and philosophical position of the faith group and provides a context for action that is part of the denomination's culture.

Many faith groups have national, regional, and local staff whose sole responsibility is in education, health, disabilities, or social justice. These staff members can provide a wealth of information and years of background in dealing with such issues within the structure and traditions of the faith group. They know what approaches work, which people are key gatekeepers, how policy is influenced and made, and which committees and personnel—from the congregational to the national level—are involved with these concerns. Some faith groups have a network of people across the country who work on concerns related to mental illness. Legitimacy is quickly established when one can point to others in the faith group who are working in this area of ministry and who have service and educational models to share.

Faith Group Policy Development. The Presbyterian Church (U.S.A.) developed an official response to mental illness in 1988. The history of that policy statement is useful in illustrating that a denomination, like a mental health organization, has an accepted way of developing policy and endorsing action in response to an area of concern.

In 1986 a consumer in Virginia and a family member in Tennessee separately petitioned their local Presbyterian regional office (the presbytery) to begin the process of passing a national resolution on mental illness for the Presbyterian Church (U.S.A.). Resolutions were introduced at the presbytery and then synod levels and finally at the national level. The task of developing an action plan at the national level was assigned to a consultant. She brought together consumers, family members, clergy, mental health professionals, and national staff to develop a resolution and background statement for presentation at the national decision-making level—the General Assembly. She organized the testimony by family members and consumers before the proper committee. When the testimony was completed, one of the committee members expressed his gratitude for the attention given this issue because he suffered mental illness. Because he feared the stigma associated with his illness, he had never shared this information with those on the committee or anyone else in the church. His statement was most moving and the resolution passed immediately. Later that week, the 200th General Assembly (The Presbyterian Church, 1988) adopted a resolution, "The Church and Serious Mental Illness," which affirmed "the ministry and mission of the church and all its people and parts with those suffering from or affected by severe mental illnesses" (The Presbyterian Church, 1988, p. 6).

This resolution and accompanying report enabled the denomination to assign staff and commit funding to develop resources and to create the Presbyterian Serious Mental Illness Network (PSMIN). PSMIN is made up of Presbyterian consumers, family members, parish clergy and chaplains, seminary faculty, medical and human service professionals, and concerned lay people. PSMIN is a constituency group within the Presbyterian Health Education and Welfare Association (PHEWA) that operates out of the Social Justice and Peacemaking Ministry Unit of the Presbyterian Church (U.S.A.).

The focus of this denomination has been on education, for example, on creating booklets for congregations, bulletin inserts, posters, pins, bumper stickers, a quarterly newsletter, and videotapes. PSMIN members and staff have had displays, workshops, and retreats at a number of Presbyterian regional and national meetings. They have developed a list of direct service programs that have emanated from Presbyterian-based congregational efforts to share with others in order to energize further activity.

Developing a Relationship with a Congregation

A relationship between a congregation and a mental health agency or organization can be invaluable in educating people about mental illness, in increasing the participation of people with mental illness in the life of the community, and in designing and sustaining programs.

Building Interest and Educating. Whatever the circumstances that spark interest in an agency or organization in developing a joint project with a congregation, the first step is to determine whether the congregation understands mental illness. It is helpful when a member of the clergy and, as often happens, one or two members of the congregation are willing to turn their attention to the issue. Those involved should assess the congregation's level of interest in programs for people with mental illness. There is an ever-increasing array of resources that a congregation can use to educate itself about mental illness and about how to respond to people with mental illness and their families. This process often begins with apparently small activities such as displaying an educational poster, placing an article in the church bulletin or newsletter, donating books to the congregation's library, or giving a sermon that mentions the need for a caring response to mental illness. These acts create an atmosphere of openness to people with mental illness. As the level of congregational education and interest grows, members of the congregation often come forward to be involved because of personal or professional interests.

A mental health agency such as a community mental health center or an organization such as the Mental Health Association can provide invaluable assistance to clergy and congregations in developing an awareness of mental illness. An agency or organization can offer to provide speakers and educational materials, opportunities for congregants to volunteer in the agency or organization's programs, and an invitation to congregants to agency or organizational functions or for a tour. It can also offer expertise about mental illness, assist clergy in pastoral care, provide professional assistance in caring for people, assist in addressing a community need, and provide assistance and expertise in developing programs (Holcomb, 1985).

Selecting a Potential Program Area. Programming can be solely focused on the population of those who have a mental illness, or it can address a wider variety of service needs. The choice of a program should fit the "art of the possible" in each congregation's situation. If a program focused solely on mental illness is not feasible in a particular setting, planners should make the choice of addressing mental illness by utilizing programs that include this issue along with others.

It is essential when establishing a project that the coordinators commit adequate time and resources for well-planned development, training, execution, and evaluation. Being flexible with time lines and meetings is particularly important when working with clergy, who have many unanticipated demands on their time.

For one congregation—Adas Israel in Washington, D.C.—a speaker was the catalyst for the development of a housing project. In 1987, as a result of a workshop on homelessness presented by Luther Place (an extensive project for homeless people based at St. Paul's Lutheran Church, also in Washington), the congregation took up the challenge of "One House of Worship—One House." A task force was organized to develop a housing program for those with mental illness. The congregation endorsed the project and agreed to support it with funds, in-kind resources, and volunteer support. Within a year the task force became an independent corporation with the agenda to create a permanent home for five women who were homeless and had mental illness. Anne Frank House opened its doors in 1988. In addition to serving the five women living in the house, Adas Israel assists other congregations to start programs that best fit their talents and capabilities by providing seed money and technical assistance.

Understanding Partnership. A constructive working relationship between a mental health organization and a congregation is built on mutual understanding, respect, and trust. Participating groups must listen to the needs of the partner organization(s); identify common goals, interests, needs, and resources; agree to resource sharing and cooperation in program development; and acknowledge limits in cooperation. One key to success is the cooperating groups' willingness to share control of the development and operation of the project. Any mental health group working with a congregation must understand that in many instances a congregation will expect to be an equal partner in the project. And the congregation may wish to play roles other than a source of referrals, a pool of volunteers, or an advocate for agency or organizational priorities. Furthermore, there must be an understanding that these relationships take time to develop. Starting slowly and understanding and respecting the limits of what can be expected from both groups is essential. Early contacts should occur without expecting any returns. This is a time to get acquainted, share information, and build mutual respect, understanding, and trust.

For example, I learned in my work with the African American Churches Task Team (AACTT) that building a cohesive group that is able to take action requires time. Initiated by two African American pastors who were part of a larger religion and mental illness network, AACTT took two years of monthly meetings before the group was willing to take on a mental health project in the community. My role, in representing the mental health community, was to sustain communication, be flexible, and encourage the group to continue its meetings and discussions. During those two years, the group educated itself about mental illness and built a strong, trusting, working relationship among the eight clergy and three mental health professionals who were the original members of AACTT. They shared pulpits, drew on one another's expertise to assist with problems of parishioners, joined in celebrations and prayer services at AACTT members' congregations, and participated in communal events such as multifaith services in conjunction with Mental Illness Awareness Week. One congregation—the Progressive Missionary Baptist Church—began a Caregivers Support Group that continues to meet weekly.

In 1993, the group was willing to embark on projects with a broader audience. The group offered three seminars for African American clergy in the St. Louis area that drew an average of seventy clergy and faith group staff per session; published a booklet of prayers, readings, devotionals, and other resources for consumers and families; offered both depression screening and educational displays at area church health fairs; and presented mental illness awareness workshops at their congregations, at other congregations, and at regional meetings of their faith groups. These efforts have increased AACTT membership and provided new leadership that will sustain the group as it continues its work.

Conducting Internal Assessments. Before committing to a joint activity, a mental health organization should do an internal assessment to identify the strengths the group brings to the project and the level of commitment of staff to working and sharing responsibility with another organization. The following areas should be covered: commitment, ability, and history of working with outside groups and volunteers; guidelines for this type of partnership effort; activity and administrative space and personnel available for the program; endorsement from those responsible for making policy; monetary and other resources needed to start up and maintain the program; local, regional, and national resources to be tapped for this project; and municipal, county, and state regulations that apply to this project (Holcomb, 1985).

Before committing to a joint program with an agency or organization, a congregation should also conduct an internal assessment. This helps the congregation identify the strengths it brings to the project and the reality of what it is able to contribute. The following areas should be covered: support and involvement from the congregation; assurance of the policymaker's (often the board's) endorsement and guidelines for this effort; history of working with outside groups; identifying activity and administrative space available for the program; and the monetary and other resources needed to start up and maintain the program. The congregation should also determine whether there are members who are willing to volunteer for this project; whether there is a commitment for paid staff to be involved; what local, regional, and national faith group or other resources might be tapped for this project; which municipal, county, and state regulations apply to this project; and what background materials (resolutions, policy statements, and so on) exist within the denomination (Holcomb, 1985).

Gaining the Support of Clergy and Religious Leaders. The support of the pastor, rabbi, or other religious leader in any undertaking in a congregation is critical. Religious leaders may not draw attention to mental illness. Ascertain how they view this issue. Their input, direction, and support is most important in presenting an image of unity of purpose; they have a particularly crucial role, in the eyes of the congregation, when a program is developed that deals with illness and grief. Clergy do not have to take a leadership role in a project, but their permission and support is critical to a project's success.

Clergy leadership was the catalyst for programming at St. John African Methodist Episcopal Church in St. Louis. The pastor, the Reverend C. Dennis Williams, attended a continuing education workshop on mental illness at Eden Seminary in 1992. He used the information provided at the workshop to develop a sermon on providing a caring response to mental illness. By preaching on mental illness, he gave permission within the community of the congregation for people with mental illness and their families to be welcomed and affirmed. Several parishioners contacted the pastor after the service to share their experiences with mental illness in their families. At the same time another parishioner—a psychiatric social worker—volunteered to take responsibility for coordinating an educational series on mental illness. Announcement of the monthly sessions was made in the church bulletin, and the educational program started. It has been operating since 1993 and is open to the community surrounding the church.

Another example of the importance of religious leadership is that of Temple Israel in suburban St. Louis. Mark Shook, the senior rabbi, had turned his attention to mental illness as a result of personal experience and involvement in a number of organizations at the local and national level. Several years ago he included a discussion of mental illness in a sermon given on Yom Kippur. He also put information about the Alliance for the Mentally Ill in the congregation's monthly mailing and posted information about mental health organizations on the congregation's community resource bulletin board. A chaplain at a local psychiatric facility learned of his interest. When a consumer approached her with the idea of starting a spiritual support group for Jewish consumers, the chaplain contacted Rabbi Shook. He agreed to meet with the consumer. They developed an agreement for Temple Israel to host the weekly meetings of the group called Achraiyut (the Hebrew word meaning "to take responsibility"). Rabbi Shook agreed to advise the group as needed. The program has been in existence since 1994. Membership fluctuates and periodically the group takes a hiatus, but it continues to meet with the support of the rabbi and others in the congregation. Rabbi Shook continues to work not only locally but at a national level by raising awareness of mental illness within the Union of American Hebrew Congregations and the Central Conference of American Rabbis.

Nurturing the Relationship. If a congregation does commit to developing a cooperative program, a solid relationship must be established between the congregation and the mental health agency or organization. A congregation can foster this relationship by attending agency- or organization-sponsored events such as an open house, inviting agency or organizational staff to describe their services to congregational or interfaith groups and clergy coalitions, encouraging members of the congregation to volunteer in the agency or organization's programs, offering congregational resources (such as space) for agency or organizational programs, and inviting agency or organizational staff to congregational functions.

Developing a Cooperative Agreement. When a mental health group and a congregation have assessed the resources they can commit to a project and are knowledgeable about a potential partner or partners, a contract or agreement should be developed. The agreement should include the rationale and commitments for developing a jointly sponsored program to meet a specific need or set of needs and for developing a working relationship to maintain the proposed program. Representatives from the congregation, whether clergy or laity, should develop the agreement with the agency director or a designee. The agency should make clear its programmatic expectations, the commitment to educate agency staff about the possibilities and advantages of working with this congregation, the contact person(s) who will be designated to meet with the congregational representatives to plan this program, and guidelines and procedures for any planned interaction with agency clients or members. The congregation should make clear its knowledge of the mental health group's mission and programs. It should also clarify its understanding of the requirements and limits of its ministry with people served by the agency or members of the organization. The agreement should acknowledge the differences in each other's perspectives, methods, purposes, goals, and objectives, in each participant's contribution to the development of the program, and in the continuing role each intends to take.

Each group should clarify its vision of the program design, of what the congregation and agency or organization expects from each other, of the regulations and contracts necessary for such a collaborative effort, of the person(s) in each organization who will have final responsibility for this project, and of the person who speaks for the organization. Knowledge of each other's channels of communication and procedures is critical and should include procedures to be used in an emergency, procedures to determine availability of facilities and equipment and how to schedule their use, ways to communicate during off-hours such as evenings, weekends, and holidays, and personnel guidelines for paid and volunteer staff liability and client confidentiality.

Other areas to discuss in such an agreement are the resources needed and available for both the start-up and continuation of the project. Agreements are needed specifying which group will provide these resources (money, personnel, space, supplies), outlining the recruitment process, and establishing the number of people who will participate in the program. When these details are not addressed, misunderstandings and lost opportunities can occur. For example, a suburban-based mental health organization approached an African American, inner-city church about the possibility of hosting an education program for families of people with a mental illness. The congregation agreed to host the program and set aside a place and dates for it. The mental health organization found two volunteer leaders for the program who agreed to work with the congregation within the projected time. However, the congregation and organization had not developed an agreement about responsibility for recruiting people to participate in the program. When the starting date was upon them, each group asked the other one, "Where are the participants?" No one had signed up to attend. The program never happened and an opportunity was lost.

Involving Volunteers. Volunteers are representatives of the larger community and are a liaison to it. They often become the best advocates for a program and its participants. The importance of a well-developed program of volunteer training cannot be overemphasized. Both initial training and follow-up support are vital to ensure that volunteer and program participants' needs are being met. Periodic meetings to provide ongoing training and support will provide advance warning of volunteer burnout.

The primary goal of a volunteer orientation program is team building. This means that a comfortable working relationship should be built among staff, program participants, and volunteers. Staff should appreciate the role of the volunteer as a person who can relate to program participants in a nonclinical manner. Volunteer orientation sessions should include information about the context and goals of the program, the history and role of the agency or organization and the congregation in the community, and the time to identify and build on volunteers' strengths and skills. Discussion of the nature of friendship and helping roles should be included. Attention should be given to listening skills, the limits of advice giving, the need to encourage responsibility rather than dependence, and the appropriate degrees of personal involvement. In developing a volunteer program, all participating groups must understand that not everyone is suited for the project. It is wise, when possible, to develop a volunteer contract that specifies the responsibilities of those coordinating the program and the volunteers. This contract should also provide information about periodic meetings for volunteers to get assistance and give input, as well as any other information essential to the particular program's operation. It must be made clear from the beginning that volunteers, and everyone else participating in the program, should not implicitly or explicitly intrude or impose their own personal biases or beliefs on participants in the program (Shifrin, Cohen, and Kraft, 1997).

Conclusion

The faith community can be a place where people with mental illness find openness and hospitality as they participate in the life of the congregation and the larger faith group. The faith community can be a place that accepts and supports both the person who is ill and the family as they face the realities of mental illness. The faith community can be a place where people who have a mental illness are valued for who they are and for how they are able to participate. This atmosphere can enable the person to feel a sense of increased self-worth, spiritual growth, and empowerment. Nancy Lee Head, who has battled schizophrenia for thirty-five years, says about her congregation: "The joy is that in congregations such as the Church of the Pilgrims, I have been given a foretaste of the Home. It encourages me to keep on keeping on in what is still, often, a painful pilgrimage" (Head, 1997, p. 15).

References

Anderson, H. "The Congregation As A Healing Resource." In D. S. Browning, T. Jobe, and I. S. Evison (eds.), *Religious and Ethical Factors in Psychiatric Practice,* Chicago: Nathan Hall, 1990.

Cunningham, F. B. "I've Got a Church in Kalamazoo." *The Journal of the California Alliance for the Mentally Ill,* 1997, (4), 26–28.

Head, N. L. "A Caring, Compassionate Faith Community." In *Caring Congregations: Observations and Commentary,* St. Louis: Pathways to Promise, 1997.

Hodgkinson, V. A., Weitzman, M. S., Kirsch, A. D., Noga, S. M., and Gorski, H. A. *From Belief to Commitment: The Community Service Activities and Finances of Religious Congregations in the United States, Findings from a National Survey, 1993 Edition,* Washington, D.C.: INDEPENDENT SECTOR, 1993.

Holcomb, W. *Building A Community Support System, A Manual for the Development of Church, Synagogue and Mental Health Agency Sponsored Support Programs for Long-Term Recipients of Mental Health Services,* Asbury Park, N.J.: New Jersey Self-Help Clearing House, 1985.

Kraft, F. "Kalamazoo, MI Congregation Includes People with SMI." *PSMIN Newsletter,* 1991, 2 (1), 7.

The Presbyterian Church (U.S.A.), "The Church and Serious Mental Illness: A Report and Resolution from the 200th General Assembly," Louisville, Ky.: The Presbyterian Church (U.S.A.), 1988.

Shifrin, J., Cohen, J., and Kraft, F. *Pathways to Partnership: An Awareness & Resource Guide on Mental Illness.* St. Louis: Pathways to Promise, 1997.

Stamp, M. "Churches Support Mental Health Ministry." *United Church News,* 1993, 9 (7), 4.

JENNIFER SHIFRIN is executive director of Pathways to Promise—a national, interfaith task force focused on ministry and mental illness. Pathways is in St. Louis, Missouri.

According to this review, religion plays a largely positive role in mental health; future research on severe mental disorders should include religious factors more directly.

Research on Religion and Serious Mental Illness

Harold G. Koenig, David B. Larson, Andrew J. Weaver

For many years, religion has been considered by some mental health professionals to be a strong contributor to mental illness (Freud, [1927] 1962; Ellis, 1980; Watters, 1992). Thus, any positive role that religion might play in the treatment of serious mental illness received little attention. Furthermore, because of the supposed incompatibility between religion and science, the relationship between religion and mental illness was largely ignored by researchers (Larson and Milano, 1997). Systematic reviews of major psychiatric journals over the past decade have demonstrated that mental health research seldom included religion, and when religion was included, it was usually measured in a brief and cursory fashion; the results were often not discussed, and relevant references were seldom provided (Larson and others, 1986; Larson, Sherrill, and Lyons, 1994; Sherrill and Larson, 1994; Weaver, Samford, Larson, Lucas, Koenig, and Patrick, in press).

In this chapter, we examine the research on the relationship between religion and severe mental illness and review research on the frequent clinical benefits and liabilities of religion in persons with comorbid medical and psychiatric illness. We also describe directions for future research, which is greatly needed in this understudied arena.

First, we describe the prevalence of religious beliefs and practices in the United States, the views of medical and psychiatric patients concerning the inclusion of the religious or spiritual dimension in their health care, and the attitudes of mental health professionals toward religion and its effects on health. Second, we survey the research on religion and severe mental illness, including the possible effects of religious practices on mental health service utilization. Third, we examine the effects that severe mental illness may have on religious beliefs and practices. Fourth, we explore the role of religion in the treatment of persons with severe mental illness and describe the role that clergy can play in caring for these patients. Finally, we examine avenues for future research in the area of religion and serious mental illness. For purposes of this review, we define the following as serious mental illnesses: bipolar disorder, recurrent severe depression, schizophrenia, and comorbid medical and psychiatric illness.

Beliefs About Religion and Health in the United States

Recent Gallup surveys indicate that 96 percent of Americans believe in God or a universal spirit, 90 percent pray, and 43 percent attend religious services either weekly or more often (Princeton Religion Research Center, 1996). The overwhelming majority of patients in health care settings also report that religious beliefs and practices are important and that they often use them to cope with the stress and problems of medical illness. This is true for patients hospitalized with a variety of health conditions (Koenig and others, 1992; Koenig, 1998).

Furthermore, consider the following: almost 80 percent of family practice patients feel that physicians should consider their spiritual needs; 37 percent want their physician to discuss religious beliefs with them; and almost half (48 percent) want their physicians to pray with them (King and Bushwick, 1994). Are these results at odds with national surveys?

Eighty-seven percent of persons answering a recent nationally representative *Newsweek* survey indicated that God answers prayers, and 79 percent said that God answers prayers for physical healing ("The Mystery of Prayer," 1997); 82 percent of respondents to a CNN/*Time* poll reported that they believed in the healing power of prayer ("Faith and Healing," 1996); 79 percent of respondents to a *USA Weekend* survey reported that spiritual faith can help people recover from illness, injury, or disease ("The New Faith in Medicine," 1996). Thus, persons in the United States with or without health problems are consistent in their belief that religion can play a very important role in their health and well-being. It is interesting that mental health professionals would have at least historically viewed such beliefs in the power of God or prayer as magical thinking. Mental health professionals may need to begin reconsidering their views about such magical thinking, given the number of people with such strong beliefs.

Attitudes of Mental Health Professionals Toward Religion

Attitudes toward religion among the general public are different from those of mental health professionals. For many years, it was thought that serious mental illness was often caused by demonic possession (Zilboorg and Henry, 1941). Today, the notion that persons with chronic schizophrenia or manic-depressive illness are possessed by demons has largely disappeared, even among many fundamentalist groups in America (Wilson, 1998).

As medicine and psychiatry began to distance themselves from religion, a number of prominent clinicians suggested that religion itself may be the cause of much neurosis and mental illness (Freud, 1927; Ellis, 1988). In fact, in a recent exposé, psychiatrist Watters (1992) suggests a direct connection between religious involvement and major mental disorders like schizophrenia and manic-depressive illness. Religious delusions are not rare in psychotic disorder and may be present in as many as 10 to 15 percent of hospitalized patients with schizophrenia (Koenig and Weaver, 1997). These delusions, however, are thought to be culturally driven—a manifestation of psychotic illness rather than necessarily a cause for it (Wilson, 1998). Persons with affective disorders may also, because of their greater capacity for affective expression, be more likely to have sudden, emotionally powerful conversion experiences (Gallemore, Wilson, and Rhoads, 1969). Given the relative dearth of scientific research in this area, the relationship between religious beliefs and practices and mental health has been the subject of heated debate among mental health and religious professionals over the last half-century.

Although mental health professionals in general have less favorable attitudes toward religion than do the patients they care for (American Psychiatric Association, 1975; Ragan, Malony, and Beit-Hallahmi, 1980), recent symposia on religion and mental health at national meetings of both the American Psychiatric Association and the American Psychological Association have been well attended. Given the increasing interest, a model curriculum for psychiatry residency has been developed (Larson, Lu, and Swyers, 1996).

The *Model Curriculum for Psychiatric Residency Training Programs* was first introduced in mid-1996 and released at the 1996 annual meeting of the American Psychiatric Association. The editorial committee was composed of psychiatrists from different religious perspectives, and they produced a course outline with both core lectures (modules) and accessory modules. The three core modules include (1) "Religion and spirituality and mental health: An introductory overview," (2) "Interviewing and assessing patients' religious/spiritual practices, beliefs, and attitudes," and (3) "Religion/spirituality in human development: A tour through the life cycle." The eight accessory modules include (1) "The psychiatry-medicine interface: Consultation-liaison (C-L) psychiatry," (2) "Collaborating with clergy in the assessment and treatment of psychiatric patients," (3) "Religious/spiritual issues in the care and treatment of substance abuse," (4) "Religious/spiritual issues in the treatment of women," (5) "Religious/spiritual issues in the treatment of abused persons," (6) "An introduction to God images," (7) "An introduction to charismatic religious experiences," and (8) "An introduction to cults and their relationship to mainstream religion."

Religious Beliefs and Spiritual Needs of Psychiatric Patients

The research concerning psychiatric patients and their religion and mental health beliefs or outcomes has lagged behind the published research concerning medical populations. Nevertheless, a few researchers have begun to examine the religiousness of psychiatric inpatients and their spiritual needs.

For example, Kroll and Sheehan (1989) studied the religious beliefs, practices, and experiences of fifty-two individuals (nineteen men, thirty-three women) admitted to a psychiatric inpatient unit in Minneapolis, Minnesota. Thirty-one percent had a diagnosis of major depression, 21 percent manic episode, 19 percent schizophrenia, 19 percent personality disorder, and 8 percent anxiety disorder. Beliefs in God (95 percent of men, 94 percent of women), the devil (74 percent of men, 76 percent of women), and the afterlife (84 percent of men, 76 percent of women) were prevalent. As far as religious practices were concerned, 47 percent of men and 55 percent of women attended church weekly and consulted the Bible or prayed before making important life decisions. With regard to religious experience, 68 percent of men and 33 percent of women reported having had a personal religious experience at some time in their lives; only 16 percent of men and 9 percent of women reported that "God or the Devil makes me do things." Patients with depression and anxiety disorder were the least religiously oriented among all patients and were also, surprisingly, the least preoccupied with sin and guilt. The authors concluded that religion plays a relatively small role in arousing the guilt that underlies depression.

Sheehan and Kroll (1990) later reported on the factors these fifty-two psychiatric patients thought might be related to their illnesses. Almost one-quarter of the sample (23 percent) believed that sin-related factors such as sinful thoughts or acts might have contributed to the development of their illness. Again, depressed patients did not appear to be preoccupied with issues involving sin and morality, and they did not believe as much as patients with other diagnoses that sin was responsible for their illness.

Lindgren and Coursey (1995) surveyed a group of thirty psychiatric patients in a psychosocial rehabilitation setting in Maryland. Diagnoses included schizophrenia (67 percent), bipolar disorder (10 percent), unipolar depression (7 percent), schizoaffective disorder (3.3 percent), personality disorder (3.3 percent), and other (10 percent). Fifty-seven percent of the patients attended religious services and reported praying at least daily. A large 83 percent (twenty-five out of thirty) felt that spiritual belief had a positive impact on their illness through the comfort it provided and the feelings it engendered of being cared for and of not being alone. Almost four in ten (38 percent) of the patients expressed discomfort with the idea of talking to their therapist about their spiritual or religious concerns.

At a Chicago medical center, Fitchett, Burton, and Sivan (1997) surveyed and compared the spiritual needs of fifty-one adult psychiatric inpatients with fifty general medical inpatients matched for age and sex. One-third of the psychiatric inpatients (39 percent) had major depression, 28 percent had a diagnosis of bipolar depression, 14 percent had schizoaffective disorder, and 20 percent had diagnoses of paranoia, alcohol or substance abuse, panic disorder, or another mood disorder. The authors reported that 80 percent of the psychiatric inpatients and 86 percent of the medical inpatients considered themselves spiritual or religious persons, with, once again, a substantial 48 percent of psychiatric patients and 38 percent of medical patients indicating that they were "deeply religious." When asked how much religion was relied on as a source of strength, 68 percent of psychiatric patients and 72 percent of medical patients indicated "a great deal," and only 10 percent of psychiatric patients and 2 percent of medical patients reported "none" or "not at all." In this study, 34 percent of psychiatric patients and 30 percent of medical patients attended religious services once a week or more, somewhat fewer than in the U.S. population.

With regard to spiritual needs, Fitchett and colleagues found that 88 percent of the psychiatric patients and 76 percent of the medical patients reported having three or more specific religious needs during their hospitalization. These needs included (1) the need to know of God's presence (84 percent of psychiatric patients and 82 percent of medical patients), (2) the need for prayer (80 percent of psychiatric patients and 88 percent of medical patients), and (3) the need for a visit from a chaplain to pray with them (65 percent of psychiatric patients and 66 percent of medical patients). Relationships between religious beliefs or practices, spiritual needs, and mental health outcomes were not examined, but it should be noted that mental health professionals have all too infrequently addressed these prevalent and important mental health needs of inpatients such as these.

Religion and Health Outcomes in Community and Medical Populations

Little research has been done on the effects of religious belief and practice on mental health outcomes in persons with chronic mental illness. What information we do have comes primarily from studies of healthy, community-dwelling persons and persons with medical illness (Larson and Larson, 1994; Matthews and Larson, 1993–1996). These studies tend to indicate that patients with extrinsic religious commitments (that is, those whose religious involvement is motivated primarily by social or personal goals and needs) have better clinical outcomes than nonreligious patients; there is a fairly strong relationship between more positive outcomes and religious participation in the community. Both epidemiological studies that assess health outcomes over time and randomized clinical trials have examined this relationship.

Epidemiological Studies. With regard to depression, several studies have reported lower rates of depression among religious persons, whether healthy (Kendler, Gardner, and Prescott, 1997; Koenig, Hays, George, and Blazer, 1997; Kennedy, Kelman, Thomas, and Chen, 1996) or medically ill (Pressman, Lyons, Larson, and Strain, 1990; Koenig and others, 1992). Kennedy and colleagues (1996) studied 1,855 older community residents (40 percent Jewish and 47 percent Catholic) in New York City (North Bronx). They found that frequent religious attendance was associated with lower rates of depression; when followed over two years, frequent attenders were less likely to become depressed, even after controlling for age, gender, health disability, and social support. Koenig and colleagues surveyed four thousand initially healthy older adults as part of the National Institute on Aging (NIA) Epidemiologic Catchment Area (ECA) survey, finding that the rate of depression in subjects who attended religious services once a week or more was only about one-half that of subjects who attended services less than once a week. This association persisted after controlling for physical health, social support, age, sex, and race.

Kendler, Gardner, and Prescott (1997) studied 1,902 female twins (mean age thirty years), finding significantly lower rates of major depression, smoking, and alcohol abuse among those who were more religious. Braam, Beekman, van Tilburg, Deeg, and van Tilburg (1997) and Braam, Beekman, Deeg, Smit, and van Tilburg (1997) have reported similar results from Europe.

Coping with Illness. When medical patients have been asked what enables them to cope with the stress of their health condition, almost 90 percent indicate that religious factors are at least moderately important in helping them to cope, and over 40 percent indicate that religion is the most important coping factor for them (Koenig, 1998). Pressman and colleagues (1990) report that among 33 elderly women hospitalized with hip fracture, greater religiousness was associated with less depression and longer walking distances at the time of hospital discharge. In a consecutive sample of 850 elderly men acutely admitted to the hospital, Koenig and colleagues (1992) found that patients who used their religious faith to help them cope were significantly less depressed; among a subgroup of 201 subjects, the extent of religious coping predicted lower depression scores six months later. The clinical effects were strongest among subjects with severe physical disability.

In a separate study, intrinsic religiousness (motivated by religion for its own sake more than for social or personal reasons) was measured at baseline in a sample of eighty-seven depressed medical inpatients; these patients were followed over time. Speed of remission from depression was increased by 70 percent for every 10-point increase on the Hoge Intrinsic Religiousness scale (Koenig, George, and Peterson, 1998). These changes were statistically significant and independent of other predictors of speed to remission, including changing physical health status. Of particular interest was the finding that among patients whose physical condition was not improving, the increase in speed of remission was 100 percent for every 10-point increase on the scale, which ranged from 10 to 50. Thus, higher intrinsic religiousness in depressed medical patients predicts faster remission from depression when these patients are carefully followed over time.

Likewise, Rabins, Fitting, Eastham, and Zabora (1990) followed sixty-two caregivers of persons with either Alzheimer's disease or recurrent metastatic cancer, examining factors that predicted adaptation two years later. A strong religious faith, along with frequent social contacts, were again the two major predictors of adaptation in this group. Religious activity has not only been found to be related to lower rates of depression and clinical maladaptation but also to less alcohol abuse (Koenig and others, 1994), drug abuse (Gorsuch,

1995), and anxiety disorder (Koenig and others, 1993). Lower anxiety in general has been less strongly connected with religious activity; there is some association with higher anxiety among those who primarily watch religious television and have lower participation in community-based religious practice. Overall, then, psychiatric problems and disorders across the board are found at lower rates among persons who are more religiously involved. This does not mean, however, that psychiatric illness, maladaptation, and serious mental pathology are not found among the religious; it only means that when large populations of people are studied, rates of mental disorder are less common among those who are religiously active.

Longitudinal Outcomes. From a physical health perspective, a number of studies have reported better physical health outcomes in persons who have a strong religious faith or are active in their religious communities. Idler and Kasl (1997a, 1997b) report on a longitudinal study of 2,812 older adults in New Haven, Connecticut. They found that frequent religious attenders in 1982 were significantly less likely than infrequent attenders to be physically disabled twelve years later—a finding that persisted after controlling for health practices, social ties, and indicators of well-being.

Religious activities have also been shown to affect mortality rates, whether following surgery outcomes or in long-term community follow-up studies. For example, Oxman, Freeman, and Manheimer (1995) followed 232 adults for six months after open-heart surgery, examining predictors of mortality. The mortality rate in persons with low social support who did not depend on their religious faith for strength was twelve times that of persons with a strong support network who relied heavily on religion. Even when social factors were accounted for, persons who depended on religion were only about one-third as likely to die as those who did not. Strawbridge, Cohen, Shema, and Kaplan (1997) report the results of a twenty-eight-year follow-up study of five thousand adults involved in the Berkeley Human Population Laboratory. Mortality for persons attending religious services once a week or more was almost 25 percent lower than for persons attending religious services less frequently; for women, the mortality rate was reduced by more than one-third, or 35 percent. Frequent attenders were more likely to stop smoking, increase exercising, increase social contacts, and stay married; even after these factors were controlled for, however, the mortality difference persisted. Findings like these counter the hypothesis that the clinical benefits of religion are "simply due" to the healthy attending religious services more frequently than the unhealthy. According to these findings, religiousness tends to *make* one healthier.

Religion and Immune Status. Koenig, Cohen, George, Hays, Larson, and Blazer (1997) have recently identified a possible biological cause for longer survival in frequent church attenders. These researchers report that frequent religious attendance in 1986, 1989, and 1992 predicted lower plasma interleukin-6 (IL–6) levels in a sample of 1,718 older adults followed over six years. IL–6 levels are elevated in patients with AIDS, osteoporosis, Alzheimer's disease, diabetes, and other serious medical conditions and is an indicator of immune system functioning. These study findings suggest that persons who attend church frequently have stronger immune systems than less frequent attenders, which may help explain why better mental and physical health have been found to be consistent characteristics of frequent church attenders.

Clinical Trials. Two randomized clinical trials have examined the effects of a religious intervention on mental health outcomes. Propst and colleagues (1992) examined the effectiveness of using religion-based psychotherapy in the treatment of fifty-nine depressed religious patients. The religious therapy used Christian religious rationales, religious arguments to counter irrational thoughts, and religious imagery. Religious therapy resulted in significantly faster recovery from depression when compared with standard secular cognitive-behavioral therapy. Surprisingly, the clinical benefits from religious-based therapy were most evident among patients who received religious therapy from *nonreligious* therapists. It had been assumed that nonreligious therapists might not be able to use religious interventions effectively.

Azhar, Varma, and Dharap (1994) randomized sixty-two Muslim patients with generalized anxiety disorder to either traditional treatment (supportive psychotherapy and anxiolytic drugs) or traditional treatment plus religious psychotherapy. Religious psychotherapy involved the use of prayer and reading verses of the Holy Koran specific to the person's situation. Patients receiving religious psychotherapy showed significantly more rapid improvement in anxiety symptoms than those receiving traditional therapy.

Religion and the Use of Mental Health Services

Because religious beliefs and activities are associated with better physical health outcomes and faster recovery from both physical and mental disorders, it would stand to reason that such behaviors might also affect the cost of health services. Few studies, however, have directly examined this effect. After studying 128 black people diagnosed with schizophrenia, and their families, Chu and Klein (1985) report that black urban patients were less likely to be re-hospitalized if their families encouraged them to continue religious worship while they were in the hospital.

A number of studies have demonstrated cost savings as a result of a chaplain intervention. In a randomized controlled trial, Florell (1973) assigned patients either to a chaplain intervention, which involved chaplain visits for fifteen minutes per day per patient, or to a control group that went about its business as usual. The chaplain intervention reduced length of stay by 29 percent ($p < .001$), patient-initiated call on registered nurse (RN) time to one-third, and use of PRN pain medications to one-third. McSherry, Ciulla, Salisbury, and Tsuang (1987) similarly report that heart surgery patients with higher-than-average personal religiousness scores on admission had post-op lengths of stay that were 20 percent shorter than those with lower-than-average scores. Bliss, McSherry, and Fassett (1995) randomized 331 open-heart surgery patients to either a chaplain intervention (Modern Chaplain Care) or Usual

Care group. Patients in the intervention group had an average post-op hospitalization that was two days shorter, resulting in an overall cost savings of $4,200 per patient.

Koenig and Larson (in press) found an inverse relationship between frequency of religious service attendance and likelihood of hospital admission in a sample of 455 older patients. Those who attended church weekly (or more frequently) were significantly less likely in the previous year to have been admitted to the hospital; they had fewer hospital admissions and spent fewer days in the hospital than those attending less often. These associations retained their significance after controlling for covariates. Patients unaffiliated with a religious community had significantly longer index hospital stays than those who were affiliated. Unaffiliated patients spent an average of twenty-five days in the hospital, compared with eleven days for affiliated patients ($p < .0001$); this association strengthened when physical health and other covariates were controlled. The implications of these results for reduction in health care costs are substantial. Similar studies are much needed in mental health services research.

Impact of Mental Illness on Religion

Serious mental illness may adversely affect religious belief and religious practice. In a study of 938 community-dwelling persons in New Haven, Lindenthal, Myers, Pepper, and Stern (1970) found that among the 753 subjects who had experienced any of sixty-two life crises, changes in church attendance were inversely related to psychopathology. Using a twenty-item measure of psychiatric functioning, they divided participants into Very Impaired, Moderately Impaired, and Unimpaired groups. Among the Very Impaired group, 20 percent reported decreased church attendance in response to stress; in the Moderately Impaired group, 11 percent reported such decreases; in the Unimpaired group, only 4 percent reported decreased attendance.

However, psychiatric functioning was positively correlated with the use of prayer during crisis. Among the Very Impaired, 58 percent used prayer during crisis; among the Moderately Impaired, 46 percent prayed; and among the Unimpaired, only 31 percent prayed. The authors concluded that when facing life crises, persons with high degrees of psychiatric impairment tended to pray more and attend church less than those with lesser degrees of psychopathology.

These findings are important in that few mental health professionals might be aware that their most impaired patients are praying more but going to church less. Not only does such a pattern make little clinical sense, in that the most impaired need to maintain contact with their social supports, but the increasing of one aspect of one's faith (prayer) with the reduction of another aspect (worship attendance) creates the potential for spiritual tension, stress, and even conflict.

Another study (Koenig and others, 1992) reports a mixed response with regard to increases or decreases in religious activity during times of increased stress. In this study of medical inpatients, researchers followed 202 medical patients for an average of six months after hospital discharge, examining the association between changing depression and changing religious coping (the seeking of comfort through religious belief and activity). The correlation was weak and nonsignificant (Pearson $r = 0.06$, $p = 0.45$). In that study, as patients became more depressed, some experienced an increase in religiousness (for example, they turned to God) and others experienced a decrease (for example, they turned away from God). On the whole, however, there was no association. These findings stress the individual variation in religious response to stress. From studies like these, for those with weak religious ties to begin with, stress often results in a reduction of interest in and dependence on religious activity; among those with strong religious ties, the opposite can occur.

Religion in the Treatment of Patients with Serious Mental Illness

Many people with serious mental illness receive treatment from the clergy. Larson and others (1988) examined the types of disorders in patients from the five National Institute of Mental Health Epidemiology Catchment Area (ECA) community surveys who sought help from clergy, compared to the types of disorders found in those who sought help from mental health professionals. Somewhat surprisingly, they found that both clergy and mental health professionals saw persons with the same severity of clinical diagnoses.

Researchers have also found that African Americans with a mental health diagnosis, especially in later life, are much more likely to seek help for their problems through clergy than through mental health specialists (Husaini, Moore, and Cain 1994). In a separate survey of 1,805 Hispanic Americans (majority Mexican, Cuban, and Puerto Rican heritage) over the age of fifty-five, researchers found that individuals were twice as likely to seek help from the church than from any other community service when addressing family problems, depression, worry, and fear (Starrett, Rogers, and Decker, 1992). In a study of 635 African American churches in the northern United States, a remarkable 38 percent of the congregations had a working relationship with the local mental health department, creating a primary link for their members to available services at all ages (Thomas, Quinn, Billingsley, and Caldwell, 1994).

Thus, persons with serious mental illness often seek out clergy for assistance in dealing with their mental health problems, and the clergy are an important source of mental health support or care for these individuals. Clergy provide psychological support, assistance with day-to-day living tasks, encouragement through prayer, and counseling guided by scripture (and psychological principles). They also enhance social support by involving these patients in religious congregational activities (Larson and others, 1988; Weaver and others, 1997).

How helpful are these clergy interventions? Although it is unlikely that religious therapies alone are sufficient to manage persons with serious mental illness, they can complement traditional therapies quite well, as shown by Propst and colleagues (1992). In our study of older medical inpatients, we found that the cognitive symptoms of depression (hopelessness, depressed mood, and so forth) were particularly less prevalent among those who depended heavily on religious belief and activity in coping, whereas the more biological or somatic symptoms of depression (weight loss, fatigue, insomnia, and so forth) were unrelated to religious coping (Koenig and others, 1995). This suggests that religious treatments are primarily beneficial for patients with milder forms of depression and that severe depression requires specialized psychiatric treatment and antidepressant drug therapy. Combination treatment that addresses psychological issues and conflicts (the mind), religious concerns (the spirit), and biological causes for mental illness (the body), may indeed harbor the potential for the best results, although little scientific research has tested such hypotheses.

Future Directions

The field of research on the relationship between religion and serious mental illness remains wide open for investigation, including genetic studies, like the work of Kendler and others (1997), that examine whether there is a shared genetic basis for religiousness (or lack thereof) and serious mental illness. There is also need for longitudinal observational studies of seriously mentally ill patients to assess the role of religion in maintaining psychosocial functioning, the more effective use of health services, and the effects of religion on mortality (as with Strawbridge and others, 1997). Studies are needed to examine differences in immune functioning between seriously mentally ill patients who are religious and those who are not, thus allowing an assessment of whether the clinical outcomes and effects are similar to those found in the studies described here.

Randomized trials are needed to test hypotheses that address whether the inclusion of religious or spiritual concerns adds something other than what is accomplished by traditional psychotherapy and medication management. This is particularly needed for those with a strong religious commitment or for those who view their faith to be the "most important" factor in their lives. Outcomes that need to be examined include not only individual patient functioning but also patient satisfaction with treatment, caregiver burden and functioning, and less traditional outcomes like stress-related growth (Park, Cohen, and Murch, 1995) and spiritual or religious growth (Pargament and others, 1990).

Finally, more studies are needed to examine the impact of religious beliefs and practices on compliance with treatment and overall cost of health and mental health care. Disorders like depression are associated with an increased use of general medical services (Koenig and Kuchibhatla, 1998). If religious beliefs or activities are associated with lower rates of depression or faster recovery from depression, then there should be a corresponding decrease in health (and mental health) service use. Although we have demonstrated that inpatient services are used less by medical patients who attend religious services frequently (Koenig and Larson, in press), these findings are preliminary. Studies are needed to examine religion's effects on service use in patients with depression or anxiety disorders, chronic schizophrenia, bipolar disorder, personality disorders, and comorbid or severe substance abuse. Indeed, we are at a research frontier that is wide open for exploration and that promises important new discoveries that may lead to better, more cost-effective treatments for patients with serious mental illness. Religious commitment has been a forgotten factor in mental health research. It would be in mental health professionals'—and their patients'—best interest to begin to examine this overlooked factor in improving patient coping as well as treatment and care outcomes.

References

American Psychiatric Association, *Task Force Report 10: Psychiatrists' Viewpoints on Religion and Their Services to Religious Institutions and the Ministry.* Washington, D.C.: American Psychiatric Association, 1975.

Azhar, M. Z., Varma, S. L., and Dharap, A. S. "Religious Psychotherapy in Anxiety Disorder Patients." *Acta Psychiatrica Scandinavica,* 1994, *90,* 1–3.

Bliss, J. R., McSherry, E., and Fassett, J. "Chaplain Intervention Reduces Costs in Major DRGs: An Experimental Study." In H. Heffernan, E. McSherry, and R. Fitzgerald (eds.), *Proceedings of the NIH Clinical Center Conference on Spirituality and Health Care Outcomes,* Mar. 21, 1995.

Braam, A. W., Beekman, A.T.F., Deeg, D.J.H., Smit, J. H., and van Tilburg, W. "Religiosity as a Protective or Prognostic Factor of Depression in Later Life: Results from the Community Survey in the Netherlands." *Acta Psychiatrica Scandinavica,* 1997, *96,* 199–205.

Braam, A. W., Beekman, A.T.F., van Tilburg, T. G., Deeg, D.J.H., and van Tilburg, W. "Religious Involvement and Depression in Older Dutch Citizens." *Social Psychiatry and Psychiatric Epidemiology,* 1997, *32,* 284–291.

Chu, C. C., and Klein, H. E. (1985). "Psychosocial and Environmental Variables in Outcome of Black Schizophrenics." *Journal of the National Medical Association,* 1985, *77,* 793–796.

Ellis, A. "Psychotherapy and Atheistic Values: A Response to A. E. Bergin's 'Psychotherapy and Religious Values'." *Journal of Consulting and Clinical Psychology,* 1980, *48,* 642–645.

Ellis, A. "Is Religiosity Pathological?" *Free Inquiry,* 1988, *18,* 27–32.

"Faith and Healing: Can Prayer, Faith and Spirituality Really Improve Your Physical Health?" *Time,* June 24, 1996, pp. 58–68.

Fitchett, G., Burton, L. A., and Sivan, A. B. "The Religious Needs and Resources of Psychiatric Patients." *Journal of Nervous and Mental Disease,* 1997, *185,* 320–326.

Florell, J. L. "Crisis-intervention in Orthopedic Surgery: Empirical Evidence of the Effectiveness of a Chaplain Working with Surgery Patients." *Bulletin of the American Protestant Hospital Association,* 1973, *37* (2), 29–36.

Freud, S. *The Future of an Illusion.* (standard ed.) London: Hogarth Press, 1962. (Originally published 1927.)

Gallemore, J. L., Wilson, W. P., and Rhoads, J. M. "The Religious Life of Patients with Affective Disorders." *Diseases of the Nervous System,* 1969, *30,* 483–486.

Gorsuch, R. L. "Religious Aspects of Substance Abuse and Recovery." *Journal of Social Issues,* 1995, *51*(2), 65–83.

Husaini, B. A., Moore, S. T., and Cain, V. A. "Psychiatric Symptoms and Help-seeking Behavior Among the Elderly: An Analysis of Racial and Gender Differences." *Journal of Gerontological Social Work,* 1994, *21* (3), 177–195.

Idler, E. L., and Kasl, S. V. "Religion among Disabled and Nondisabled Elderly Persons: Attendance at Religious Services as a Predictor of the Course of Disability." *Journal of Gerontology,* 1997a (Nov), *52B,* S306–S316.

Idler, E. L., and Kasl, S. V. "Religion among Disabled and Nondisabled Elderly Persons: Cross-sectional Patterns in Health Practices, Social Activities, and Well-being." *Journal of Gerontology,* 1997b (Nov), *52B,* S294–S305.

Kendler, K. S., Gardner, C. O., and Prescott, C. A. "Religion, Psychopathology, and Substance Use and Abuse: A Multimeasure, Genetic-epidemiologic study." *American Journal of Psychiatry,* 1997, *154,* 322–329.

Kennedy, G. J., Kelman, H. R., Thomas, C., and Chen, J. "The Relation of Religious Preference and Practice to Depressive Symptoms Among 1,855 Older Adults." *Journal of Gerontology,* 1996, *51B,* P301–P308.

King, D. E., and Bushwick, B. "Beliefs and Attitudes of Hospital Inpatients about Faith Healing and Prayer." *Journal of Family Practice,* 1994, *39,* 349–352.

Koenig, H. G. "Religious Attitudes and Practices of Hospitalized Medically Ill Older Adults." *International Journal of Geriatric Psychiatry,* 1998, *13,* 213–224.

Koenig, H. G., Cohen, H. J., Blazer, D. G., Pieper, C., Meador, K. G., Shelp, F., Goli, V., and DiPasquale, R. "Religious Coping and Depression in Elderly Hospitalized Medically Ill Men." *American Journal of Psychiatry,* 1992, *149,* 1,693–1,700.

Koenig, H. G., Ford S., George, L. K., Blazer, D. G., and Meador K. G. "Religion and Anxiety Disorder: An Examination and Comparison of Associations in Young, Middle-aged, and Elderly Adults." *Journal of Anxiety Disorders,* 1993, *7,* 321–342.

Koenig, H. G., George, L. K., Meador, K. G., Blazer, D. G., and Ford, S. M. "The Relationship between Religion and Alcoholism in a Sample of Community-dwelling Adults." *Hospital and Community Psychiatry,* 1994, *45,* 225–231.

Koenig, H. G., Cohen, H. J., Blazer, D. G., Kudler, H. S., Krishnan, K.R.R., and Sibert, T. E. "Cognitive Symptoms of Depression and Religious Coping in Elderly Medical Patients." *Psychosomatics,* 1995, *36,* 369–375.

Koenig, H. G., and Weaver, A. J. *Counseling Troubled Older Adults: A Handbook for Pastors and Religious Caregivers.* Nashville, Tenn.: Abingdon Press, 1997.

Koenig, H. G., Hays, J. C., George, L. K., and Blazer, D. G. "Modeling the Cross-sectional Relationships between Religion, Physical Health, Social Support, and Depressive Symptoms." *American Journal of Geriatric Psychiatry,* 1997, *5,* 131–143.

Koenig, H. G., Cohen, H. J., George, L. K., Hays, J. C., Larson, D. B., and Blazer, D. G. "Attendance at Religious Services, Interleukin–6, and Other Biological Indicators of Immune Function in Older Adults." *International Journal of Psychiatry in Medicine,* 1997, *27,* 233–250.

Koenig, H. G., George, L. K., and Peterson B. L. "Religiosity and Remission from Depression in Medically Ill Older Patients." *American Journal of Psychiatry,* 1998, *155,* 536–542.

Koenig, H. G., and Larson, D. B. "Use of Hospital Services, Church Attendance, and Religious Affiliation." *Hospitals and Health Services Administration, Southern Medical Journal,* in press.

Koenig, H. G., and Kuchibhatla, M. "Use of Health Services by Hospitalized Medically Ill Depressed Elderly Patients." *American Journal of Psychiatry,* 1998, *155,* 871–877.

Kroll, J., and Sheehan, W. "Religious Beliefs and Practices Among 52 Psychiatric Inpatients in Minnesota." *American Journal of Psychiatry,* 1989, *146,* 67–72.

Larson, D. B., Lu, F. G., and Swyers, J. P. (eds.). *Model Curriculum for Psychiatry Residency Training Programs: Religion and Spirituality in Clinical Practice.* Rockville, Md.: National Institute for Healthcare Research, 1996.

Larson, D. B., and Milano, M.A.G. "Making the Case for Spiritual Interventions in Clinical Practice." *Mind/Body Medicine,* 1997, 2 (1), 20–30.

Larson, D. B., Pattison, E. M., Blazer, D. G., Omran, A. R., and Kaplan, B. H. "Systematic Analysis of Research on Religious Variables in Four Major Psychiatric Journals, 1978–1982." *American Journal of Psychiatry,* 1986, *143,* 329–334.

Larson, D. B., Hohmann, A. A., Kessler, L. G., Meador, K. G., Boyd, J. H., and McSherry, E. "The Couch and the Cloth: The Need for Linkage." *Hospital and Community Psychiatry,* 1988, *39,* 1,064–1,069.

Larson, D. B., and Larson, S. S. *The Forgotten Factor in Physical and Mental Health: What Does the Research Show?* Rockville, Md.: National Institute for Healthcare Research, 1994.

Larson, D. B., Sherrill, K. A., and Lyons, J. S. "The Neglect and Misuse of the *R* word: Systematic Reviews of Religious Measures in Health, Mental Health, and Aging." In J. S. Levin (ed.), *Religion in Aging and Health: Theoretical Foundations and Methodological Frontiers.* Thousand Oaks, Calif.: Sage, 1994.

Lindenthal, J. J., Myers, J. K., Pepper, M. P., and Stern, M. S. "Mental Status and Religious Behavior." *Scientific Study of Religion,* 1970, *9,* 143–149.

Lindgren, K. N., and Coursey, R. D. "Spirituality and Serious Mental Illness: A Two-part Study." *Psychosocial Rehabilitation Journal,* 1995, *18* (3), 93–111.

Matthews, D. A., and Larson, D. B. *The Faith Factor: An Annotated Bibliography of Clinical Research on Spiritual Subjects.* Vols. 1–4. Rockville, Md.: National Institute for Healthcare Research, 1993–1996.

McSherry, E., Ciulla, M., Salisbury, S., and Tsuang, D. "Spiritual Resources in Older Hospitalized Men." *Social Compass,* 1987, *35* (4), 515–537.

"The Mystery of Prayer: Does God Play Favorites?" *Newsweek,* Mar. 31, 1997, pp. 56–65.

"The New Faith in Medicine: Believing in God May Be Good for Your Health, According to the Latest Research." *USA Weekend,* Apr. 5–7, 1996, p. 5.

Oxman, T.E., Freeman, D.H., and Manheimer, E.D. "Lack of Social Participation or Religious Strength and Comfort as Risk Factors for Death After Cardiac Surgery in the Elderly." *Psychosomatic Medicine,* 1995, 57, 5–15.

Pargament, K. I., Ensing, D. S., Falgout, K., Olsen, H., Reilly, B., Van Haistsma, K., and Warren, R. "God Help Me: Religious Coping Efforts as Predictors of the Outcomes of Significant Negative Life Events." *American Journal of Community Psychology,* 1990, *18,* 794–824.

Park, C. L., Cohen, L. H., and Murch, R. L. "Assessment and Prediction of Stress-related Growth." *Journal of Personality,* 1995, *64,* 71–105.

Pressman, P., Lyons, J. S., Larson, D. B., and Strain, J. J. "Religious Belief, Depression, and Ambulation Status in Elderly Women with Broken Hips." *American Journal of Psychiatry,* 1990, *147,* 758–759.

Princeton Religion Research Center. *Religion in America.* Princeton, N.J.: The Gallup Poll, 1996.

Propst, L. R., Ostrom, R., Watkins, P., Dean, T., and Mashburn, D. "Comparative Efficacy of Religious and Nonreligious Cognitive-behavior Therapy for the Treatment of Clinical Depression in Religious Individuals." *Journal of Consulting and Clinical Psychology,* 1992, *60,* 94–103.

Rabins, P. V., Fitting, M. D., Eastham, J., and Zabora, J. "Emotional Adaptation Over Time in Care-givers for Chronically Ill Elderly People." *Age and Ageing,* 1990, *19,* 185–190.

Ragan, C., Malony, H. N., and Beit-Hallahmi, B. "Psychologists and Religion: Professional Factors and Personal Belief." *Review of Religious Research,* 1980, *21,* 208–217.

Sheehan, W., and Kroll, J. "Psychiatric Patients' Belief in General Health Factors and Sin as Causes of Illness." *American Journal of Psychiatry,* 1990, *147,* 112–113.

Sherrill, K. A., and Larson, D. B. "The Anti-tenure Factor in Religious Research in Clinical Epidemiology and Aging." In J. S. Levin (ed.), *Religion in Aging and Health: Theoretical Foundations and Methodological Frontiers.* Thousand Oaks, Calif.: Sage, 1994.

Starrett, R. A., Rogers, D., and Decker, J. T. "The Self-reliance Behavior of the Hispanic Elderly in Comparison to Their Use of Formal Mental Health Helping Networks." *Clinical Gerontologist,* 1992, *11,* 157–169.

Strawbridge, W. J., Cohen, R. D., Shema, S. J., and Kaplan, G. A. "Frequent Attendance at Religious Services and Mortality Over 28 Years." *American Journal of Public Health,* 1997, *87,* 957–961.

Thomas, S. B., Quinn, S. C., Billingsley, A., and Caldwell, C. "The Characteristics of Northern Black Churches with Community Health Outreach Programs." *American Journal of Public Health*, 1994, *84*, 575–579.

Watters, W. W. *Deadly Doctrine*. New York: Prometheus Books, 1992.

Weaver, A. J., Samford, J. A., Kline, A. E., Lucas, L. A., Larson, D. B., and Koenig, H. G. "What Do Psychologists Know About Working with the Clergy? An Analysis of Eight APA Journals: 1991–1994." *Professional Psychology: Research and Practice*, 1997, *28* (5), 471–474.

Weaver, A. J., Samford, J. A., Larson, D. B., Lucas, L. A., Koenig, H. G., and Patrick, V. "A Systematic Review of Research on Religion in Four Major Psychiatric Journals: 1991–1995." *Journal of Nervous and Mental Diseases*, in press.

Wilson, W. P. "Religion and Psychosis." In H. G. Koenig (ed.), *Handbook of Religion and Mental Health*. San Diego: Academic Press, 1998.

Zilboorg, G., and Henry, G. W. *A History of Medical Psychology*. N.Y.: Norton, 1941.

HAROLD G. KOENIG is associate professor of psychiatry and director of the Center for the Study of Religion/Spirituality and Health, Duke University Medical Center, Durham, North Carolina.

DAVID B. LARSON is president of the National Institute for Healthcare Research in Rockville, Maryland, and adjunct professor of psychiatry, Duke University Medical Center.

ANDREW J. WEAVER is a clinical psychologist at the Hawaii State Hospital and a member of the clinical faculty, Department of Psychology, University of Hawaii, Kaneohe.

Support for writing this chapter was provided by the John Templeton Foundation, Radnor, Pennsylvania.

On theoretical, clinical, and research levels, there are many ways to attend more fully to spirituality and religion in developing and implementing mental health programs.

Recommendations for Integrating Spirituality in Mental Health Services

Roger D. Fallot

Although there have been many movements to bring spirituality and religion into more fruitful relationships with personality theory, psychotherapy, and general clinical practice in the mental health professions, the role of spirituality in the lives of people with severe mental disorders and in the services provided for them has been relatively neglected. As the preceding chapters have demonstrated, however, greater consideration of spirituality in programming for people with serious mental illness is feasible, justifiable, and increasingly important to a comprehensive view of the whole person in cultural context. Developing spiritually responsive programs enriches the depth and breadth of clinical thinking and service provision and expands the resources available to consumers. For mental health agencies and professionals who wish to incorporate the spiritual dimension of consumers' experiences more fully in their work, there are numerous opportunities to do so. This concluding chapter briefly summarizes some key recommendations in conceptual, clinical, and research arenas.

The Theoretical Level

On the theoretical level, conceptions of the commonly adopted biopsychosocial model need to be expanded to include more explicitly spiritual aspects of experience. Whether thinking about services at the individual or systems level, the spiritual dimension is increasingly important to a holistic and culturally competent clinical approach. This is especially true and most obvious for those consumers who readily identify themselves as spiritual or religious. However, as many functional definitions of spirituality remind us, it is both possible and clinically helpful to consider the experiences of all consumers from a spiritual perspective. In order to do this, of course, spirituality must be understood in an inclusive and expansive way, that is, conceptualized broadly enough to be useful in understanding not only the experiences of the self-identified religious individual but of all consumers. Definitions of spirituality that give priority to functional issues have a clear advantage in achieving this necessary level of generalization.

Clinicians can understand the importance of spirituality in a person's life by emphasizing the way the person finds or constructs a sense of meaning or purpose, the way core values are enacted in everyday behavior, the way ultimate questions are asked and experiences of ultimate reality understood, the way a sense of belonging and community is expressed, or the way optimal functioning is achieved. Spirituality may indeed be connected, for some individuals, to a specific organized religious tradition, but it should not be conceptually restricted in this way. On the contrary, many central motifs in humanistic, existential, and transpersonal psychology, as well as in psychosynthesis and in mind-body-spirit integrative work (to name just a few), tap this dimension with clarity and power.

The Clinical Level

At the clinical level, the most direct implication of this view is the development and use of assessment approaches that include the spiritual dimension (see Chapter Two). Many models have been developed and published; it is important to choose or formulate one that is appropriate to the sociocultural realities of the consumers involved, to agency and provider interests, and to the service planning that follows from the assessment. (The most important dimensions of a spiritual assessment in a program centered on psychotherapeutic interventions, for example, may differ from those in one prioritizing vocational and social goals.)

Including spirituality in service planning, then, grows from adequate assessment. As outlined in Chapter Two, in collaborative planning and shared decision making with consumers, spiritual *problems, goals,* or *resources* may be involved. Once a specific concern or goal is identified, the clinician and consumer can then discuss how best to address this area. For instance, if a consumer identifies a problem involving conflict between his or her religious activities and some other goal, the clinician may then explore with the consumer various ways to resolve this conflict. Is it an issue to discuss in psychotherapy or in consultation with a religious professional or by simply changing one of the goals? Clinicians who feel inadequately trained in spiritual issues should be reassured that they do not need to become experts in spirituality to be more attuned to its importance in service planning. They do need to be empathic with the spiritual experiences of consumers and open to weaving these experiences into a holistic approach to services.

Clinicians often need, in addition, to become more fully aware of the broad network of community activities involving spirituality and religion and to develop a more differentiated view of these activities so that referrals can be made with specificity and sensitivity. Just as effective referrals to other human services are based on a shared effort to find the best fit among consumer needs and preferences, the services involved, and the particular provider, so may discussions about spiritual needs revolve around expanded knowledge of the community's resources and the most appropriate fit for the consumer's goals. Developing active relationships with faith communities (shared programs, mutual referrals, education) is one step in expanding clinicians' sense of the universe of possibilities. Increased knowledge of the tremendous variety of spiritual and religious specialists also makes referral and collaboration more effective.

Mental health agencies may also decide to offer services related to spirituality in their own programs. Individual or group interventions with specifically spiritual goals are not necessarily outside the purview of mental health services (see, for example, DSM-IV's category of religious or spiritual problems). As Kehoe (see Chapter Five) has demonstrated, the discussion of religious issues may be well integrated in a broader psychosocial program. Questions of group leadership (mental health professionals, religious professionals, consumers, or some combination of these) and membership (open or closed, homogeneous or heterogeneous) can be answered only after the group's goals, content, and process are specified. The important distinction between settings in which the activities of an organized religion are discussed and those in which they are enacted needs to be maintained. Services whose goals are to cultivate hope, clarify life direction and purpose, or make decisions about responsibility and forgiveness may all be considered relevant to the spiritual needs of consumers.

Other services may be sensitive to spiritual concerns without taking them as a primary focus. Here the role of the mental health professional is to listen actively and attentively for the ways spiritual issues emerge in other contexts. For example, in trauma recovery work among people with severe mental disorders, the need for including spiritual resources is not uncommon. As the group addresses whole-person concerns, discussions of the reasons for suffering, of making sense of violence, of forgiveness and its value, and of revenge and its appropriateness may frequently be in the foreground. By taking these questions seriously and exploring rather than minimizing them, group leaders or individual clinicians may facilitate greater clarity in seeing how spirituality fits with the recovery process.

The Research Level

Finally, at the research level there is ample justification for the inclusion of religious variables in mental health services research (see Chapter Eight). Researchers have developed increasingly sophisticated measures of religious or spiritual dimensions (moving beyond simple reports, for example, of involvement in religious activities to numerous inventories and rating scales of the type and style—the "how"—of spirituality). With these measures come improved methods for distinguishing not only the central associational relationships among spirituality and key outcomes but for examining a variety of validity questions as well. Longitudinal research affords an especially appropriate opportunity to examine the timing and causal relationships among spiritual or religious variables and a variety of core mental health outcomes.

A wide range of evidence, then, supports increased attention to spiritual dimensions of experience in theory, assessment and service planning, service development and delivery, and research. Enriching mental health services in these ways means offering more comprehensive and integrated approaches to the multiple needs and interests of consumers, clinicians, and researchers.

ROGER D. FALLOT *is co-director of Community Connections in Washington, D.C., and a member of the adjunct faculty in pastoral counseling at Loyola College in Maryland.*

INDEX

Back Issue/Subscription Order Form

Copy or detach and send to:

Jossey-Bass Inc., Publishers, 350 Sansome Street, San Francisco CA 94104-1342

Call or fax toll free!

Phone 888-378-2537 6AM-5PM PST; Fax 800-605-2665

Back issues: Please send me the following issues at $25 each.
(Important: please include series initials and issue number, such as MHS80.)

1. MHS _____

_____

_____

$ _____ Total for single issues

$ _____ Shipping charges (for single issues **only**; subscriptions are exempt from shipping charges): Up to $30, add $5^{50} • $30^{01}–$50, add $6^{50} $50^{01}–$75, add $7^{50} • $75^{01}–$100, add $9 • $100^{01}–$150, add $10 Over $150, call for shipping charge.

Subscriptions   Please ❑ start   ❑ renew my subscription to *New Directions for Mental Health Services* for the year 19___ at the following rate:

❑ Individual $63   ❑ Institutional $105

NOTE: Subscriptions are quarterly, and are for the calendar year only. Subscriptions begin with the spring issue of the year indicated above. For shipping outside the U.S., please add $25.

$ _____ Total single issues and subscriptions (CA, IN, NJ, NY, and DC residents, add sales tax for single issues. NY and DC residents must include shipping charges when calculating sales tax. NY and Canadian residents only, add sales tax for subscriptions.)

❑ Payment enclosed (U.S. check or money order only)

❑ VISA, MC, AmEx, Discover Card #_____ Exp. date_____

Signature _____ Day phone _____

❑ Bill me (U.S. institutional orders only. Purchase order required.)

Purchase order #_____

Name _____

Address _____

_____

Phone_____ E-mail _____

For more information about Jossey-Bass Publishers, visit our Web site at:
www.josseybass.com   **PRIORITY CODE = ND1**

Other Titles Available in the New Directions for Mental Health Services Series

H. Richard Lamb, Editor-in-Chief

MHS36 Improving Mental Health Services: What the Social Sciences Can Tell Us, *David Mechanic*

MHS33 Barriers to Treating the Chronic Mentally Ill, *Arthur T. Meyerson*

MHS14 The Young Adult Chronic Patient, *Bert Pepper, Hilary Ryglewicz*